North Carolina Women *of the* Confederacy

Original text written and published by
Mrs. John Huske (Lucy London) Anderson
Fayetteville, N. C.
Historian, North Carolina Division
United Daughters of the Confederacy
1926

Revised Edition
Updated and compiled by the Cape Fear Chapter #3
United Daughters of the Confederacy
2006

North Carolina Women of the Confederacy
Revised edition © 2006 Cape Fear Chapter #3,
United Daughers of the Confederacy

The 1926 text is reprinted here with permission of the heirs of Lucy London Anderson and updated by the present editors. Additional material is supplied by the publisher and chapter members Mary Ann Barrett, Brenda Birmelin, Pat Gasson, and Polly Sheats.

Published by Winoca Press for the Cape Fear Chapter #3
United Daughters of the Confederacy
Wilmington, North Carolina

On the cover and title page: Portrait of Rose O'Neal Greenhow, engraved from a photograph by Joseph Brown and published by Richard Bentley, London, 1863.

Printed in the United States of America

13 14 15 16 17   5 4 3 2

LIBRARY OF CONGRESS CATALOGING-IN-PUBLICATION DATA

Anderson, Lucy London.
   North Carolina women of the Confederacy / original text written and published by Mrs. John Huske (Lucy London) Anderson ; updated and compiled by the Cape Fear Chapter #3, United Daughters of the Confederacy.—Rev. ed. / updated and compiled by the Cape Fear Chapter #3, United Daughters of the Confederacy.
   p. cm.
   Includes index.
   ISBN-13: 978-0-9755910-7-9
   ISBN-10: 0-9755910-7-X
   1. North Carolina—History—Civil War, 1861–1865—Women. 2. United States—History—Civil War, 1861–1865—Women. 3. Women—North Carolina—History—19th century. I. United Daughters of the Confederacy. Cape Fear Chapter No. 3. II. Title.
   E573.A26 2006
   973.7082'0975—dc22

                                                          2006001930

WWW.WINOCA.COM

CONTENTS

A Note on the Revised Edition .... Page v

First Confederate Monument in North Carolina .... Page viii
Dedicative .... Page 1
Foreword .... Page 3
North Carolina Women of the Confederacy .... Page 5
The Mothers of Many Inventions .... Page 8
Women Take Men's Places .... Page 11
Secret Service Work .... Page 14
Women Prepare for War .... Page 21
Blockade Running into Wilmington .... Page 41
Women in Nursing and Hospital Work .... Page 45
Picture of a Yankee Foraging Party .... Page 56
Courage Displayed .... Page 57
Canteen Work .... Page 68
Other Incidents of Women's Work .... Page 71
Heroic Women of Western North Carolina .... Page 86
Wit and Repartee .... Page 93
Literary Women of the Sixties .... Page 98
Christmas During the Confederacy .... Page 107
Women Urge Church Bells for Confederate Cannon .... Page 110
Other Characters of North Carolina .... Page 114
Founder of North Carolina Division of the U.D.C. .... Page 119
Young Women Take Men's Places .... Page 124
Recollections of Young Girls .... Page 126
First Confederate Flags Made by North Carolina Women .... Page 132
First Monuments and Memorial Associations .... Page 144
North Carolina Mothers of Many Sons .... Page 153
Welcome Home, Heroes in Gray .... Page 166
North Carolina Verses of the Sixties .... Page 171

Index .... Page 179

A NOTE ON THE REVISED EDITION

In the decades following the War between the States many communities and groups—in the North and South alike—sought to memorialize their sacrifices and preserve their histories. Such memorials took the form of markers and monuments, days of remembrance, and, as in this volume, books containing recollections, stories, and verse.

Lucy Worth London Anderson, wife of John Huske Anderson of Fayetteville, North Carolina, undertook in the 1920s to record episodes in the history of the Confederate women of her state. As North Carolina historian of the United Daughters of the Confederacy she was in an advantageous position to collect, edit, and publish these, and she did so in 1926, using the services of a local printer, Cumberland Printing Company of Fayetteville.

By now the book has been out of print for some time, and copies have become rare. It is the wish of the Cape Fear Chapter #3 of the UDC to make Lucy London Anderson's work available again, widely accessible for research or enjoyment.

This project was the special interest of past chapter president Mary Ann Tilden Barrett, who held the office from 1998 to 2004 but passed away before she could see the book through the press. The Cape Fear Chapter has carried the work to completion and now dedicates this volume to honor her memory.

A great deal of historical research and scholarly publication on the women of the War between the States—Northern and Southern, black and white, wealthy and poor—has been undertaken since this small book was first published. Mary Elizabeth Massey's *Bonnet Brigades* (1966; later *Women in the Civil War,* 1994); Drew Gilpin Faust's *Mothers of Invention: Women of the Slaveholding South in the American Civil War* (1996); *The Women's War in the South: Recollections and Reflections of the American Civil War* (1999), edited by Charles G. Waugh and Martin H. Greenberg; and Laura F. Edwards's *Scarlett Doesn't Live Here Anymore: Southern Women in the Civil War Era* (2000) all examine the roles of Confederate women in greater detail, and with greater distance.

Nonetheless, Mrs. Anderson's book was one of the first to record the stories of North Carolina Confederate women, and for that reason it remains a valuable resource. Though Mrs. Anderson states that her material is "well authenticated," the absence of notes and bibliography in the original makes it an overwhelming task to verify her sources, and no claim to scholarly rigor is made for this edition. Likewise, in keeping with the goal of reproducing a text that is a relic and evidence of its times, none of the terms or concepts that may appear appallingly biased or demeaning today have been modified.

This entirely new setting of type, however, should make the text far easier to read than in older printings. Obvious typographical errors have been corrected, missing or erroneous words have been supplied [generally in brackets], and poems and quotations have been revised to agree with original sources wherever feasible. Grammar, spelling, and mechanics have been slightly revised according to today's preferences, with an aim to clarify for modern readers—while intruding as little as possible into the author's original text.

Perhaps most useful, an index of personal and place names has been added (missing first names and other facts in the text have been researched and supplied wherever possible). It is our hope, and that of the Cape Fear Chapter #3 of the United Daughters of the Confederacy, that the 2006 edition will prove interesting and edifying to a new generation of readers.

THE PUBLISHERS

THE FIRST CONFEDERATE MONUMENT
IN NORTH CAROLINA

Erected by the WOMEN of Fayetteville, December 30, 1868
In Cross Creek Cemetery

INSCRIPTION
Nor shall your glory be forgot while fame her record keeps,
For honor points the hallowed spot where valor proudly sleeps.

IN LOVING REMEMBRANCE

This Volume Is Dedicated
to
North Carolina's Women
of the
Confederacy

"Whose loving ministrations nursed the wounded
   to health,
And soothed the last hours of the dying;
   Whose unselfish labors
Supplied the wants of their defenders in
   the field,
Whose unwavering faith in our Cause
   Showed ever a guiding star,
Through the perils and disasters of war;
   [Whose] sublime fortitude
Sustained them under every privation and
   All suffering;
Whose floral offerings
   Were yearly laid upon the graves of those
Whom they loved and honored;
      and
Whose patriotism
   Has taught their children
To emulate the deeds of their Confederate sires."

(From the "Women of the South" Supplement.)

FOREWORD

In presenting this little volume to the people of my State, I do so with the hope that this may be the beginning of a REAL HISTORY of the part the women of North Carolina took in the Confederacy. It is with great happiness that I am realizing a "dream come true," in the publication of these few sketches I have collected, which illustrate the history of North Carolina's women of the Confederacy. The many delightful friendships that I have made in trying to discover our women of the Sixties in various communities have more than repaid me for the hundreds of letters written. Many more names and incidents could have found a place here if all the sections of the State had responded to my call for facts about the women of the Confederacy.

These stories that have been recorded are well authenticated, but the collection of these was like digging in the undug earth for hidden gold, hard to find, but very precious when discovered.

My grateful appreciation is given to those who have allowed me to share their memories, and to turn back the pages of history with them.

To be a Daughter of the Confederacy is the greatest honor we can pay our Confederate ancestry, and it is the sacred duty of each member of this beloved organization to fulfill the first object of the constitution of the North Carolina Division, which is

"To honor the memory of those who served and those who fell in the service of the Confederate States . . . also to recall the part taken by Southern women in patient endurance of hardship and patriotic devotion during the struggle, as in untiring efforts after the war during the reconstruction of the South."

What prouder heritage can we give our children than these records? Every land cherishes its memories, and history is nothing but memories, so when every Daughter of the Confederacy awakens to the importance or preserving these records we will have a history of our State that will fill VOLUMES.

We may prove worthy descendants of these noble women of the Sixties, and in remembrance of them let us strive for their steadfastness and courage. "Their brave deeds shall brightly shine upon the books of FAME, and Time's immortal scroll will keep the record of their names."

Lucy Worth London Anderson.
Fayetteville, N.C.
August 23rd, 1926.

NORTH CAROLINA WOMEN
OF THE CONFEDERACY

"The loving mothers, sisters, sweethearts, wives,
Who, when the war drum's fatal summons came,
Gave up the dearest treasures of their lives
And bore the Martyr's cross in Freedom's name."

The spirit displayed by those women of the Confederacy was worthy of the wives and mothers of the grandest heroes who ever fought on the field of battle.

The women of North Carolina in the Confederacy possessed the same courageous and self-reliant spirit, that was inherited from this state's Colonial and Revolutionary women, who acted with their men in shaping some of the most important events in the establishing of the United States of America.

We point with pride to the fact that North Carolina women were the first to resist the unjust tax of England, in the Edenton "Tea Party"; that our state made the first open resistance against the Stamp Act; that the first battle of the Revolution was in Alamance County; that the first Declaration of Independence was signed (May 20, 1775) by the patriots of Mecklenburg County; that at Halifax was assembled the first Provincial Congress, which instructed delegates to stand for Independence; and that at the [Revolutionary War] battle of Moore's Creek was fought the first real victory for the colonies. In the War between the States North Carolina has a proud heritage which should be handed down to the remotest generation—for did we not give *more* men to the cause and lost more than any other Southern state? The women of our state point with pride to the fact that North Carolina was "First at Bethel, farthest at Gettysburg and Chickamauga, and last at Appomattox."

So much the greater pride we should feel for these women of our State of the Sixties, who are much closer in blood to our women of today than those of one-hundred and fifty years ago, and we should pass on the individual story of the self-sacrifice and courage of North Carolina's woman of the Confederacy.

"Let us preserve her memory and keep fresh,
Like flowers in dew, her noble deeds."

Though it was with sorrowing hearts they saw North Carolina leave the Union, yet when her State's rights were violated and their beloved State threatened by hostile foe, they showed the resolute spirit of their pioneer "mothers" when they took their stand beside their Confederate soldiers in the fight for State sovereignty.

That the women of our State today may better appreciate and value the character and achievements of the women of the Confederacy, it is my privilege to give glimpses of these women, and I have tried to record a bit of their history, from 1861 to 1865, a great part of which is unwritten.

To attempt to portray as well as our imperfect records permit, the spirit, character, and deeds of the North Carolina women of the Confederacy is a difficult task, for so little has been preserved as to the part individual women of the state played in the war.

Their noblest eulogy is a simple portrayal of their character and work. The noble heroism of these women showed itself in uncomplaining suffering, in loving ministration, and in the efficient discharge of arduous duties.

Many eulogies have been given to the women of the Confederacy, but these pages are simply to resurrect a few names and incidents which could be duplicated in every section of the State. North Carolina women of the Sixties! Who shall call one a heroine more than the other, for all worked in the same way to the same end! "The humblest soul who does her bit, in God's own book of Life is writ."

The way our women of the Sixties rose to meet the emergency of war should place her name high in the State's hall of fame.

Every community had her heroine, and its special story of splendid daring, endurance, and achievement should be put on record. The story of the ingenious devices and clever makeshifts to supply needful things during the years of blockade and non-production; the ills and atrocities of Reconstruction; the records of Soldier's Aid Societies, Wayside Hospitals, and Memorial Associations; sketches of everyday life in the Confederacy—its lights and shadows, fun, work, jokes, songs, costumes, and fare—all these are of great value in preserving for a history of these women in each section of North Carolina.

THE MOTHERS OF MANY INVENTIONS

"Our mothers wove of cornshuck braid
Their hats and baskets too,
Of homespun all their dresses made,
Those testing days of '62."

The women were in truth "The mothers of many inventions," and in every locality of this state and of the South there was shown the same resourcefulness in manufacturing household articles. Hats were fabricated from palmetto leaves, cornshucks, oat straw, and broad-leaved grasses, buttons made from gourds, clothes fastened with buttons of persimmon seeds, slippers made from rabbit and squirrel fur and old tent canvas. Much of the underwear, blankets, towels, jeans, and clothing for the soldiers were made at home by spinning or weaving. Everything was utilized. Cartridge belts and boxes were made from layers of cloth sewed together and covered with varnish.

The fur of rabbits was mixed with a small amount of cotton and carded and spun into thread and made into stockings and gloves.

Roots, bark, leaves, and twigs of trees were used for dye with a small amount of copperas or bluestone, which was carefully preserved. A kind of clay was used for dye.

Shoes were made of cowhides in the natural state and were blacked with soot taken from the bottom of iron pots used in cooking over the fire. Cloth uppers were made by the women themselves when the soles of worn-out shoes were in good condition or had enough foundation to re-sole.

The best and warmest of the cloth was made into clothes for the men, and a clean suit was always on hand in case any of them should come home.

The necessity developed all their latent ingenuities, as they had to find substitutes for food such as sugar, coffee, soda, and tea. Sorghum was used for sugar; rye, wheat, and okra for coffee; ashes of corn cobs for soda; and any suitable dried leaf for tea, such as sassafras and blackberry.

Such household necessities as candles were made by placing drippings in a pan with a woolen rag for the wick. Pine knots were also used. Soap was made by boiling scraps of meat, meat-skins, and bones in lye, obtained by placing wood ashes in a keg or barrel, or any wooden vessel, and dripping water through.

Tea and coffee were sweetened with sorghum molasses. Christmas fruit cake was made for the soldiers out of dried cherries, dried whortle berries, candied watermelon rind, and molasses.

When beeves disappeared and there was no tallow for candles, sycamore balls were soaked in fat and burned in pans for lights, or strings twisted hard were put in bottles filled with grease or beeswax. Ink, colored with indigo or berry juice, was made from oak and cedar balls. Old scraps of wallpaper gummed with flour paste served to carry tender messages to soldiers far away. Our women of the Sixties were pharmacists as well as chemists. They compounded from herbs many simple remedies for their children and servants, when there was no medicine to be had. Nitre for gunpowder was often dug by the women from old smokehouses and tobacco barns.

Wool from old mattresses was often recarded and spun into yarns for socks to keep the soldiers from having cold feet. Carpets, heavy curtains, and draperies were unraveled and woven into blankets for the army. In answer to a call for silk for war balloons, discarded silken dresses were pulled apart and the silk furnished. Garments discarded years before were made over for indefinite service. The homespun cloth which was woven at home was a uniform for men, women, and children. To relieve its ugliness the women concocted dyes of various kinds from poke berries and elder berries, and some of these dresses were far more prized than formerly had been the brocades and satins. These Confederate girls wore them proudly, singing the patriotic song of the South:

> "My homespun dress is plain I know,
> My hat's palmetto too;
> But then they show what Southern girls
> For Southern rights will do."

WOMEN TAKE MEN'S PLACES

"Hear ye not the sound of battle,
Sabres clash and muskets rattle?
Fight away, fight away, fight away in Dixie Land."

At the advent of war our women had to take up the burdens dropped by the absent fathers and brothers, and with real ability they assumed control of plantations, stock, and slaves and financed the homes and industries of the state. Many women of wealth joined the poorer women in tilling the fields and reaping the harvests, as many of the slaves joined the Federals. The fact that these women, in a great part, kept the state fed attests their ability, and during the last months of the war, almost the entire army of General Lee was fed by North Carolina. The burdens imposed on these capable women increased each day, and additional responsibilities were assumed.

A few months before Lee's surrender, news reached central North Carolina that his army was without food. At once, in houses both humble and stately, the women made a division even to the last peck of meal, and with no thought of themselves the contribution to the army was shipped. When a tax was levied by the state for whatever remained in the storehouse or crib, the women met the tax with little evasion. Nothing was a sacrifice for these women, when relieving the wants of their soldiers.

When the first N.C. Hospital was equipped and opened at Petersburg in October 1861, under Doctor Peter Hines of Raleigh, from among the women of this state who offered their services as nurses three very efficient ones were chosen. They were Mrs. [William (Catherine DeRosset)] Kennedy of Wilmington, Mrs. Beasley of Plymouth, and Miss M. L. Pettigrew of Raleigh.

In almost every neighborhood they organized sewing societies, knitting associations, hospital aid societies, and nursing clubs. In many places churches were turned into hospitals and were depots for bolts of cloth, linen, and flannel. Sewing machines ran day and night. At railroad junctions such as Raleigh, Goldsboro, Greensboro, Charlotte, Salisbury, Weldon, and Fayetteville, wayside hospitals equipped with surgeons, medical supplies, and rude operating tables were established, with the women volunteering as nurses. Countless women went from house to house distributing cloth to be sewed and yarns to be woven and then collected and shipped as offerings to their soldiers. After an arduous day women often worked far into the night, adding comfort to their soldier boys who were fighting for the land they loved.

The women and girls made the haversacks and knapsacks of leather bound with braid, also the heavy coats worn by the men, fully equipping companies of soldiers. The girls knitted hundreds of pairs of socks, made knapsacks, knit mufflers, gloves, wristlets, and havelocks (helmets), and were busy every moment. Then there were the "good things" put up in boxes and sent to camp—pies, etc.—each article meaning real self-denial by those at home.

We had a "Molly Pitcher" right here in our own State, Mrs. L. M. Blalock, disguised as a Confederate soldier. She, with her husband, on May 20, 1862, joined the 26th North

Carolina Regiment as a recruit from Caldwell County, and was supposed to be a young brother of her husband. She served nearly a year and took regular soldier fare, being in three big battles. Not one of the company suspected she was a woman till, her husband being discharged on account of sickness, she disclosed her identity and resigned.

SECRET SERVICE WORK

*"God shares the gift of head and heart,
And crowns blest woman with a hero's part."*

One of the most outstanding heroines that North Carolina can claim in the War between the States was Miss Emmeline Pigott of Carteret County. This young woman's name deserves a high place among our State's bravest women, for her cool courage was often shown in the midst of great danger. At the beginning of the war, Miss Pigott, then a young girl, had given her whole heart to the cause of the South, nursing the sick and wounded soldiers who were brought in from the attacks on our coasts. Her soldier sweetheart fell in the battle of Gettysburg, and after that Emmeline Pigott felt that she must do even more for the Confederacy. She offered herself for secret service work in the Confederate government and bore important dispatches in large pockets adjusted under her full skirts. Many dangerous journeys were made by her between New Bern (which was occupied by the Yankees) and the seaports, and she narrowly escaped capture very often, going through great danger to fulfill her mission.

Finally this daring young girl was seized, and while being searched, she chewed up and swallowed the important message which she had concealed on her. If this had been discovered she would have been shot as a spy. She was imprisoned at

New Bern and while there an attempt was made on her life by the administering of chloroform through her prison window.

Friends worked hard to free her, but without success, but at length she sent for some influential men in New Bern whom she knew were traitors, telling them if she were brought to trial she would disclose things that would cause them to suffer. So their influence was brought to bear with the Federal authorities and she was released without a trial. The name of Emmeline Pigott is held in the highest veneration, and the Morehead City Chapter of the U.D.C. is named in her honor. To the end of her eighty years no cause was so dear to her as the Confederacy.

Heroines of New Bern

"When the darkening storm of danger gathers round,
There woman, with undaunted faith and courage brave, is found."

When New Bern was captured by the Yankees, the women who had not escaped, suffered greatly. The story of New Bern's capture, and the suffering of its women, is told by Mrs. F. C. Roberts, a daughter of Mr. J. C. Cole, one of the most loyal of Confederates. Mrs. Roberts says, "Those who remained in New Bern could hear nothing from their loved ones, outside the town, (as the Federals were occupying New Bern) except through the underground mail."

With all their vigilance the Federal troops could not discover who delivered this mail, and who received it. Governor Stanley, an old "personal and political friend of her father" (Mr. J. L. Cole) obtained permission for Mrs. Alexander Taylor to go freely about the town and to visit the prisoners and relieve the wants of the poor sufferers confined in the prisons. She had many false pockets and somehow into them the daily mail crept.

On one occasion a Federal officer joined her in the street; he said, "Mrs. Taylor, it is very strange, but we cannot find out how or where this Rebel mail comes in or who receives it." Her heart was in her throat; she thought her last hour had come, and she would be shot as a spy, but she determined to die game, so she said, "Why, I receive it and at this moment my pockets are full of letters; would you like to see them?" It passed as a joke, but it was rather risky, and had they been found on her, her life would have paid the forfeit.

Mrs. Taylor visited the prison daily and ministered to the unfortunates there—often going hungry that she might have some delicacy to take them. She was called "The Prison Mother," and many a poor captive called her blessed. Among these was a lady from Beaufort who barely escaped being shot as a spy. (This was Miss Emmeline Pigott, whose thrilling story has been recorded.)

Mrs. M. C. Cole and Mrs. [Alexander] Taylor, accustomed all their lives to ease and luxury, tended their own gardens, rolled the wheelbarrow, dug with spade and hoe, and raised vegetables for their own tables and to sell. And while they did this the Federal soldiers sat on the fences and ridiculed them, calling them "gal" and "aunty" and "mama."

Mrs. Elizabeth Carraway Howland also rendered valuable aid when New Bern was captured, in sending out specifications of the forts the Yankees were making and other information to our troops. She would secret the paper in a small roll inside the bone of a ham which her small daughter and son carried down the river to the Confederates. The little girl would present a bouquet of flowers to the captain of the

Federal gunboat, and she would be allowed to pass without being searched.

This splendid woman, who had studied medicine with her father, doctored the Confederate prisoners ill with yellow fever in New Bern, and not one of her patients died, though the Yankee doctors lost hundreds. She was a prison angel, secretly clothing and feeding these destitute sufferers.

These New Bern women not only suffered persecution by the Yankees, but went through a terrific scourge of yellow fever, caused by quantities of meat being allowed to decay on the scorching wharves. They nursed the ill and then assisted in burying the dead. Mrs. Julius Lewis (before her marriage, Abigail Hart) kept Northern officers in her home to get from them news for the Confederacy. If she had been found out she would have been shot as a spy.

Mrs. A. M. Meekins ran the blockade into New Bern to ascertain for General Lee the exact strength of the Federal forces there before the Confederates' attack on Fort Fisher. Disguised as a country woman with a bale of cotton to sell, with her ready wit she secured the desired information and passed safely back through the Union lines.

Among the splendid women of New Bern Miss Mary Attmore is an outstanding figure, not only for her memorial work after the war, but for her indomitable courage and forceful character during the capture of New Bern. When this town had been taken by the Yankees Miss Attmore, as one of the most prominent of its women, was kept as one of the hostages to insure the safety of the Federals within, as they were in constant fear that New Bern would be fired on by troops without. In spite of the protests of her relations Miss Attmore refused to leave her home, but lived alone without fear. Twice she was almost choked to death by "bummers" who were intent to plunder, but [she] miraculously escaped. In the gray of an early morning she awoke to find several Yankees digging up the graves in the family burial ground on her estate. Without hesitation or calling for help, this independent woman with great dignity of learning appeared amongst the marauders, commanding them to put down their shovels at once, exclaiming, "Is it possible that you could be guilty of such a dastardly trick as to dig open the graves of our ancestors!" The men, to the amazement of neighbors who witnessed the scene, not only removed their caps, but began replacing the earth on the graves and departed, leaving this free-spoken and courageous woman in possession of her dead.

By her ready wit, free speech, and fearlessness she compelled the admiration of her captors and was allowed greater liberty than the other residents of New Bern.

Though a cultured and refined Southern woman, Miss Mary Attmore possessed characteristics of a general in her command of the most terrible situations, showing the spirit of her revolutionary ancestor, Thomas Attmore.

The president of the North Carolina Division, United Daughters of the Confederacy, Mrs. J. Dolph Long, Hannah Attmore by birth, is the great-niece of this intrepid woman of the Sixties.

> "God shares the gift of head and heart,
> And crowns blest woman with a hero's part."

There is an unknown heroine of New Bern whose intrepid daring is worthy of record, though her name was not disclosed by Col. Stephen D. Pool, the narrator of this incident in Clark's *N.C. Histories*. Col. Pool says that in November '62, he was ordered to Trenton, N.C., to capture a Federal train. In the early morning hours an elderly country man dashed up on a fastly ridden horse and delivered to him a paper, which on being opened, appeared to be blank. The rider said that a young girl had ridden alone to his door in the darkness of night and delivered this note and told him to take it at full speed to any Confederate officer at Trenton, as it contained important information.

Col. Pool applied to the seemingly blank sheet of paper a hot iron, the heat bringing out the writing (probably written with milk). It said that the Federal general had returned to New Bern two days sooner than anticipated and was to leave that very morning with a force accurately detailed on the paper, on an expedition to burn the railroad bridge at Weldon. The object of Col. Pool's plans being thus frustrated, he returned at once to Kinston and gave the officer in command the information which he had secured through the daring of this loyal girl of the Confederacy. Such an array of troops was placed in front and upon the flanks of the Federal general as to cause him to rapidly retrace his steps.

The lady requested that her name not be told, but it was found that she was one most tenderly reared and very young, and her night ride at great personal risk to convey this important information was greatly appreciated by the Confederates. This is the only story of a woman of the Confederacy recorded in the State's regimental histories amongst the daring deeds of the men of North Carolina.

The little five-year-old daughter of Mrs. Corbett, Mary Bailey Murphy, with unusual foresight for a child, hearing that Sherman's soldiers were coming, had begged her mother to let her hide her own silver spoons and forks (old family silver, which had been given her by her grandmother). So this plucky little girl of the Sixties dug up her box which had been buried beside that of her mother's, and hid it herself, and this was the only hidden treasure that the bummers did not find. This silver is one of her treasured possessions today, this little girl being now Mrs. Beaman, the beloved Superintendent of the North Carolina Confederate Woman's Home.

WOMEN PREPARE FOR WAR

"And when our rights were threatened, the cry rose near and far."

Every community had its soldier's aid and knitting societies, and each mother, wife, sweetheart, and sister looked after her own dear ones on the field and constantly sent comfortable clothing and boxes of food to them from their own depleted larders.

We cannot mention many of these societies, but facts concerning some have been secured.

Recollections of Fayetteville Women

After the United States Arsenal at Fayetteville was taken by the Cumberland County Militia, April 22, 1861, the women of Fayetteville returned to their serious work of finishing the equipment of their soldiers for the terrible work before them, that of WAR. A reminiscence written by Miss Sarah Ann Tillinghast just after the war ended gives us a vivid picture of how the young girls did their part in the war work. She says: "The school girls were wild; no use was it to mention books to them; it was their plain duty to sew for the soldiers, and sew they did, though I must say that some of their work might have been criticized by particular persons. There were dress parade suits and fatigue suits to be made as well as underclothing suitable for camp life—tents, haversacks, canteens to be covered, in fact every part of the outfit except the knapsacks was made by the volunteer labor of the women. They assembled in bees from house to house, where the most experienced ladies could oversee the difficult parts of the work, such as the making of the coats which could be trusted to no novices. And when our first two companies left us, we felt that they were as well provided for as soldiers could expect to be, and we girls were proud to feel that we had done our part as well as school girls could be expected to.

"What wonderful triumphs of genius were then achieved by the ladies in the 'reconstruction' of old dresses, in 'making claise auld claise look as maist as weels' the new.' How garrets were ransacked for old discarded garments that were brought out and surprised by having a fresh lease on life given them in new characters. What nice bonnets were made of old black silk dress bodies, trimmed with goose feathers and lined with red or blue satin from the lining of old coat sleeves, hats constructed of old discarded ones of feathers, trimmed with old coats' collars and cock's plumes cut off the rooster in the yard. Space fails me to tell of all the 'shifts' that were made—not that we thought so much of our personal appearance as in happier times, but women will always try to 'look decent' at least, and young girls will not often be found too sad to refuse to consider the set of a dress or the becomingness of a hat.

"But through all the privations, real or relative, not one of us ever thought of the possibilities of giving up. To the bitter end we believed firmly in the justice and final success of the cause, and even after the devastation of Sherman's army we did not lose hope, but thought 'some way' would be found out of the difficulty.

"The surrender of Lee came upon us like a thunderclap. We refused to believe it. 'Lee surrendered!' 'Lee would never surrender.' Women are so unreasonable, they can't see what they don't want to see really. We begged the soldiers not to give up. It could not be possible that the South was subdued. We wept and wrung our hands. 'March on to death or victory!' was our cry.

"The war had ended as we had never believed possible; all the days of agonizing suspense our wives, mothers, sisters, and sweethearts had endured, while their loved ones were hourly exposed to deadly danger, the nights of sleepless anxiety, wishing yet dreading for the morning—all the privations, self-denials, losses, had been in vain. All the precious lives had been sacrificed, and defeat at last, overcome by overwhelming numbers. Desolation met our eyes all around. What was lurking among us? The earth seemed turned upside down, and chaos seemed to reign.

"But not long did North Carolina lie weeping in the dust. 'Twas not in her nature. She gathered herself up and went to work again.

"But though our generation may not realize it, I believe we can see the dawning of a new day, and our children will be better and nobler men and women for all we have gone through, and we will be able to understand that the war *was not in vain.*"

Miss Alice Campbell, another young woman active in the war-work of Fayetteville, gives an account of the "Return of the Bethel Horses" of Cumberland County and the welcome they received from the citizens of this old Scotch settlement.

"Our military companies, the honored old Fayetteville Independent Light Infantry (with their motto emblazoned on their flag, 'He that hath no stomach to this fight let him depart'), and the LaFayette Light Infantry, with ranks full of true men, were coming home after their enlistment for the first six months of the war. We women, thinking this was the end of the war, had been making preparations for two weeks to welcome our boys home. Oh, the happy hearts and the tears of joy that were shed over our dear boys in gray, who had returned in safety to their loved ones. This was of short duration, for every one of them went into the service again, and the terrible struggle began in earnest.

"We women spun, wove, and knitted thousands of socks and gloves for our soldiers. (Note: Miss Campbell used the same knitting needles for the boys of the World War that she used for the boys in gray. She was the president of the Young Woman's Knitting Society in the Sixties.)

"I had a calico dress for State occasions for which I paid ten dollars a yard and shoes that cost one hundred dollars a pair; we paid ten dollars a pound for sugar and tea, and later it could not be bought for any price. The women were busy from early morning till dewy eve.

"As the years passed so slowly and our forces were being diminished daily our faith was still firm that victory would at last be ours."

Early in the war a number of ladies of Fayetteville formed the "Cumberland County War Association." The minutes of this organization show a wonderful amount of work accomplished, as it included assistance to the needy families of the soldiers at the front. Many valuable contributions from adjoining counties were received and dispensed by the women of Cumberland.

A large amount of socks was dispensed through the association contributed by the "Young Ladies Knitting Society" and the "Juvenile Knitting Society." The children were not idle in doing their bit. The girls from ten to thirteen years old knitted socks and if they didn't finish at least one pair every two weeks, they were fined ten cents. Two little boys belonged to this society and each one knitted a pair of socks every two weeks.

Letter From the Front

This unique letter is an expression of appreciation from the "boys in gray:"

"Camp near Petersburg,
"February 16th, 1864.

"The members of the third company Battalion, Washington Artillery of New Orleans, embrace this opportunity of tendering to the 'Young Ladies Knitting Society' of Fayetteville, N.C., their thanks for the recent present of sixty-five pair of socks.

"Exiled from home as we are, and debarred by the exigencies of war from the attention and care of the loved ones at home such attentions are peculiarly gratifying and when the grim visage war shall hide his wrinkled front and halcyon days of peace shall have returned to bless our distracted country, we shall tell our mothers and sisters of their goodness and they will unite us in thanking them.

"For all the socks the maids have made,
Our thanks for all the brave;
And honored be your pious trade,
The soldier's sole to save."

Women of Wilmington

"And all we know is that they gave
A sweetness to the days now dead,
For they were kind and they were brave."

Mrs. Armand J. DeRosset, of Wilmington (born Eliza Lord), was one of our women of the Sixties who was endowed with such administrative ability that it was often said of her, "She should have been a general." Under her direction the Soldiers' Aid Society was early organized, and for four years did its work with unabated energy. While her six sons were fighting, Mrs. DeRosset assisted her husband in his medical work, nursing the sick, being keenly active to the needy. With the valuable assistance of the women of Wilmington (especially Mrs. Alfred Martin, who was vice-president), large supplies were made and kept on hand. Canvas bags were made to be filled with sand and used in the fortifications at Fort Fisher. Canteens were covered, haversacks made, also cartridges for rifles, and powder bags for the great columbiads were made by the hundreds.

Mrs. DeRosset had a large room in her own home fitted up as a store room, seizing every chance to secure supplies through the blockade. Many a soldier blessed these women for comforts bestowed on them. Men still live who treasure the War Bibles given them, as among their most valuable possessions.

Mrs. DeRosset's ability to overcome difficulties in getting all she needed for the men was the constant wonder of those who assisted her. The following is an incident of her executive power. After the first attack of Fort Fisher the garrison, in great peril, was to be reinforced with Junior Reserves. The wires brought the news that in a few hours they would arrive, hungry and footsore. Mrs. DeRosset was asked if the ladies could feed them; the ready reply came, "Of course we can." And through the energy and resource of herself and assistants, she proved equal to the task.

They nursed through the harrowing scenes of hospital life, and tenderly buried the dead. When all was over this band of faithful women, in July, '66, organized a permanent memorial association with the purpose of rescuing from oblivion the names and graves of the gallant soldiers who are buried in and near Wilmington.

The sick soldiers in the hospital at Fort Fisher were supplied with nourishing food and nursed by women who courageously remained there. The wife of Major [James M.] Stevenson and her sister, Mrs. Mary F. Sanders, were among those who helped to make these Confederates more comfortable, though in constant personal danger themselves. The Soldiers' Aid Society in Wilmington did a wonderful work for this hospital, supplying clothes, covering, and quantities of provisions.

When Wilmington was occupied by the Yankees the Rev. A. A. Watson was ordered to change the prayer of the Protestant Episcopal Church for the Confederate States and to pray for the president of the United States instead of the president of the Confederate States. This the rector refused to do. Whereupon Gen. [Schofield] seized the Church buildings, had all the pews and the pulpit torn out and removed, and had the building converted into a hospital. Also the Methodist church on Front Street was seized and turned over to a negro congregation.

It was on Ash Wednesday that the Yankees turned the congregation out of St. James Episcopal Church. The following lines ([based on] the 79th Psalm) were written on that day in the Bible of Mrs. William Lord. "The heathen have entered our land, they have spoiled our heritage, they have closed the doors of our sanctuary, shut the mouths of our prophets, despoiled us of our privileges, refused to obey the voice of God who has said—'Call the people together proclaim a solemn feast; our people weep, the ministers sigh.' And our cry is O Lord subdue our enemies, restore unto us our poor suffering stricken servants, the blessed means of grace and let not our sins cry for vengeance against us. Give us grace and faith to have submission to Thy holy will and so improve these sore afflictions that they tend to Thy honor and glory and the good of our immortal souls. Amen. Eliza Hill Lord."

Mrs. Robert H. Cowan, of Wilmington, suffered a most thrilling experience while refugeeing near Laurinburg. Surrounded by Yankees, with two of her children at the point of death, she was subjected to every conceivable indignity. They pulled the rings from her fingers while holding her sick child and kicked the cradle of the other child with the brutal remark, "That one is dead already," while one rested his loaded gun against Mrs. Cowan's chair. The gang of marauders, yelling and cursing, slapped the face of the aged grandmother as he pulled the watch chain from her neck. Another ruffian threw his arm around a young daughter, saying he had just come out of the penitentiary, which they could well believe. With the sick babies, Mrs. Cowan, with her mother and young daughters (afterwards Mrs. Junius Davis, Mrs. James I. Metts, and Mrs. Louis DeRosset) escaped during the night to an old hut, where they lay hid while the negro regiments and greater part of Sherman's army passed. Just the terrible experiences of this one family would be sufficient to show what the women of the Sixties endured.

Capt. S. A. Ashe, in his monumental [Biographical] *History of North Carolina*, gives many pathetic incidents of the hopes and fears of the women of our State during this critical and heartrending period. His story of North Carolina as a scene of warfare in the Confederacy is of gripping interest, and from it we have a vivid picture of those days when the women behind the lines showed their unflinching bravery. Capt. Ashe mentions the fact that Sherman in a letter to his wife, December 16, 1864, (taken from the Great March) by Sherman's aide-de-camp Maj. Nichols, said: "We came right along, living on turkeys, chickens, pigs, bringing along our wagons loaded as they started with bread, etc. I suppose Jeff Davis will have to feed the people of Georgia now instead of collecting provisions of them to feed his armies.

"The amount of burning, stealing and plundering of our army makes one feel ashamed of it."

Maj. Nichols goes on to say in the Story of the Great March, "Almost every inch of ground in the vicinity of the dwellings was poked by ramrods, pierced by sabres or upturned by spades. It was comical to see a group of red bearded veterans punching the unoffending earth. Nothing escaped the observation of the sharp witted soldiers."

Capt. Ashe tells of a visit of Gen. Sherman, while in Fayetteville in March '65, at the home of Col. Frederick Childs, the commandant of the Arsenal. There resided the colonel's sister, Jennie, Mrs. Anderson, and his aged mother, from whose house at Fortress Monroe Sherman had been married. The venerable lady was somewhat afflicted with palsy.

When the general entered he said: "Ah, this is no place for you. You must go to Gen. Woodbury's (one of her daughters was the wife of the distinguished engineer Gen. Woodbury of the United States Army). I am sorry to see you here. But as to that damn little Fred Childs—if I catch him I'll hang him as high as Haman." And, then, in a wild burst of passion, he exclaimed: "I come through now creating devastation. If that does not answer I will come through with fire and sword, and slay the people and leave desolation; and then if they do not submit, I will come through again, and leave nothing alive and sow the ground with salt." And the palsied widow of Gen. Childs looked on aghast in horror at the spectacle.

The Yankee troopers came upon the home of Mrs. Duncan Murchison in Cumberland County and, in spite of protests, burst in the room of a young girl who was in the last stages of typhoid fever. The child was taken from the bed in which she lay and died while the bed and the room were being searched for money and jewelry. Although over seventy years old Mr. Murchison, in spite of the pleadings of the women of his family, was dragged half clad to the nearby swamps, where he was compelled to stay until the raiders had left. Every act of vandalism was committed on this plantation, but the Murchison women bore it all with heroic fortitude.

Mrs. John McDaniel of Cumberland County not only had her home burned by these soldiers, but her husband was carried out into the woods and hanged to a tree in order to make him give up secrets of his valuables. His death was prevented by some of his faithful servants and family, who rescued him from this terrible fate. The home of Mrs. Thomas McDaniel in this same community was also burned after the soldiers had taken it as their sleeping place for the night; this was certainly a very ungracious way of returning "hospitality"(?). Both of these homes were ransacked and the furniture and all valuables demolished or stolen. The Yankees as they set fire to this residence were heard to exclaim exultingly: "Well, we've burnt up another home of a d_____ rich old Rebel."

A most unusual tribute is given to a plucky woman of the Sixties of Wake County, being an inscription on her tombstone. She lies buried in a little churchyard at Fuquay Springs, near Raleigh. This is the inscription:

> "Here lies Mrs. Eliza Ann Jones,
> A devoted Christian Mother,
> Who whipped Sherman's bummers
> While trying to take her dinner
> Pot, which contained a hambone being
> Cooked for her soldier-boy."

Women of Old Hillsboro

> "There's a pedestal high in the hall of my heart,
> For the Women of Dixie Land,
> Who nobly and proudly played their part,
> With a courage superbly grand."

The women of Hillsboro were among the most active of our State. The late Col. Benehan Cameron loved to recall how as a little boy on his pony he would assist his mother, Mrs.

Paul Cameron, an ardent Southerner and daughter of the distinguished Thomas Ruffin, in acting as messenger boy for the Ladies Aid Society. Though too young to enter the army (which he longed to do) this youngster did his part and always felt that he belonged to the Veterans.

Miss Rebecca Cameron (Honorary Historian of the North Carolina Division U.D.C.) gives this glimpse of the women's work in Hillsboro during the war:

"Mrs. William A. Graham (wife of ex-Governor Graham), who gave five sons to the Confederacy, was president of the soldiers' aid society of Orange County. I think Mrs. Kate Roulhac (daughter of Hon. Paul Cameron) was vice-president, and Miss Annie Roulhac was the secretary. Our records were all kept in the Court House, and when the Yankees came they burned all of them. The aid society used to meet every week at the Court House and work for the soldiers and their dependent families. A committee was formed of which my mother, Mrs. William Cameron, was chairman and executive, of ladies who would send food for the troop trains as they passed by the Hillsboro depot. A committee of ladies would go to the depot with their servants and board the train and feed the men, who had their tin cups and plates in their haversacks. Mr. Tom Webb was president of the North Carolina Railroad, and he gave us a standing pass for all the trains passing here. After much experience of the difficulties of the work, my mother devised the plan of going down to Morrisville on the train going east, and feeding the men on board, then getting off at Morrisville with baskets, papers, etc., going into the waiting room and there making the divisions into separate bundles, and on our way back to Hillsboro giving the packages to the men on board. These men were generally sick and wounded, though sometimes they were being transferred to other places or commands. Hillsboro soon became known as a feeding station, and the conductors would tell us how eagerly the men would inquire when they would reach this town. Mrs. W. A. Graham always sent her carriage and her servant to carry us to the depot and back home. Our horses had gone into the service with father's battery, THE ORANGE LIGHT ARTILLERY. A four-gun battery was made out of the bells of the Episcopal, Presbyterian, and Baptist churches. These bells were sent to the Tredegar iron works in Richmond to be cast into cannon. They were said to be the finest metal sent to the iron works.

"My oldest brother, Donald Moore Cameron, enlisted at the age of fourteen, in father's battery.

"In the midst of the sorrow and the work for our soldiers, when the men came home on furlough or were stationed near us, we girls laughed, danced, rode, and sang with our boys. We bore ourselves with a gay high courage, though often we were starving at home, even as they were starving at the front."

Another glimpse of Hillsboro in the Sixties is given me by that distinguished Christian educator of today, Mrs. Lucy H. Robertson, of Greensboro, whose mother, Mrs. Katherine Watkins Owen, was active in the soldiers' aid society of Hillsboro. Mrs. Robertson says, "I was a very young girl in Hillsboro at the time of the war, though old enough to be interested in what was going on. Hillsboro was intensely Southern in its sympathies, and every woman seemed to be doing all in her power to help the beloved cause. The Soldiers' Aid Society was very active in all kinds of war work, sewing garments, knitting socks, furnishing food, looking after the sick or wounded soldiers passing by this little town on the trains going by daily. Committees of ladies took turns in carrying coffee, buttermilk, and other things suitable for the convalescents or others able to leave the hospitals and return to their homes. I used to go with my mother and her committee, and was very proud to be permitted to pour the buttermilk into tin cups so eagerly held out by the weak and trembling hands to receive the refreshing drinks. They all seemed so appreciative of these little attentions—so pitifully little compared to their great sacrifice. Another little service I, and other young people, were permitted to render was converting our mother's table and bed linens into lint to go to the hospitals, for our women were always alert to everything that might alleviate the sufferings of our soldiers. Many were the boxes packed in Hillsboro by that Aid Society to go to the front to add something to the comfort of our brave men. As I remember her, my mother was a tireless worker, with many other of like spirit in all these activities."

Women of Goldsboro

"Hurrah, hurrah, for Southern rights, hurrah."

The women of Goldsboro saw war from early in 1862, and were active in their soldiers aid hospital work. A wayside hospital was established here, and the women were organized in committees for nursing. Gen. Gatlin established his headquarters at Goldsboro, so the girls of the town enjoyed the society of the young Confederates in his command. Several battles were fought around this section: first the battle of Kinston, December, '62, when the Federals were endeavoring to capture Goldsboro (where was won the last Confederate victory in the war); then the fight of Whitehall not far from Goldsboro; then Gen. Foster's raid on Goldsboro itself. The result of all this fighting was to fill Goldsboro with many wounded soldiers, and every available place in the city was used by the women. The female college of Goldsboro overflowed with the sick and wounded, the young girls assisting the older ones in their tender administrations.

The town was again occupied by the Federals when Sherman's army was around Bentonville after that battle. Here was enacted the same act of destruction as characterized all of Sherman's march.

Mrs. John Slocumb of Goldsboro, one of the "true and tried," said that it was heart-rending to daily see crowds of country women with their babies in their arms coming into town to beg food and shelter, after Sherman's raid. Sherman himself ordered from his home (so that he might occupy it) an aged citizen with a family of eighteen children and grandchildren, most of them females.

Washington Women

A "Military Sewing Society" was formed on the 23rd of April, 1861, by the women of Washington, N.C., with Miss M. M. Hoyt as president and Miss Margaret De Mille, secretary. Resolutions were adopted and sent to the captain of each company of their county to confer with the ladies as to the most efficient and immediate services they could render, and it was resolved, "That the ladies highly approve of the course the gentlemen have pursued in so promptly responding to the needs of the country and preparing to fight her battles."

The following note to Capt. Spannor shows the solicitude of these women.

"Should there still be members of your company not suitably provided for you will very much oblige the ladies by making known to them their wants and we will take great pleasure in giving them our prompt attention.

"Yours with great respect, Sir.

M. M. Hoyt."

The following incident is in a letter of Gen. W. A. Blount of Beaufort, written by his nephew Capt. Roman of Washington, N.C. He says:

"A great many, perhaps 300, of the Georgia regiment are sick with measles and typhoid fever. About six hospitals have been taken charge of by the ladies, who tend the sick and spare no pains. Aunt (the late Miss Patsy B. Blount) has taken three into her house, and nurses them constantly. She generally has six soldiers to eat with her—I believe she would give them her last rag of clothes—and the other ladies are not much behind her. The rooms of Miss Fannie Owen are used as a hospital."

Women of Mecklenburg County
(Where the last meeting of the Confederate Cabinet was held)

"Hold up your heads, indulge no fears,
For Dixie swarms with volunteers.
Fight away, fight away, fight away in Dixie Land."

As the tales of suffering poured in from the various encampments, rousing the mothers, wives, and sweethearts to make themselves useful in this great crisis, the women of

Charlotte, on August 28th, '61, formed an association for relief and aid, composed of sixty-five ladies, called the "Soldier's Aid Society of Charlotte," adopting a formal constitution, which is a most interesting document. The meetings were held in a room given by Mrs. J. H. Carson. The number of garments made during the first year was over three hundred, which was a large amount when most of the work was by hand. This society distributed thousands of dollars worth of goods, not only to the soldiers in the field but for their destitute families at home. In writing of this work Mrs. M. A. Osborne (one of the officers of this Soldier's Aid Society) says, "May the light diffused more abundant grow, for the glory dies not as the grief is past." Out of this society later in the Sixties was formed the Ladies Memorial Association, with Mrs. Osborne [as] president, and Mrs. John Morehead, secretary. This beautiful service to our Confederate dead has been carried on by the daughters of these patriotic women.

There was a Confederate Hospital on South Tryon Street, in Charlotte, on the site of the old fairgrounds, which buildings were used to care for the wounded soldiers in the spring of '65. Many died there and were buried in the old field back of the fairgrounds. Some time afterwards, Mrs. John Wilkes superintended the removal of their bodies to a spot in Elmwood Cemetery.

A meeting of the Confederate Cabinet was held at the home of Mr. and Mrs. Wm. F. Phifer. Mrs. Phifer was hostess to Gen. Beauregard and his staff while they were in Charlotte in the spring of '65, and owing to the illness of Mr. Trenholm, Secretary of the Treasury, who was also a guest in this home, the cabinet meeting was held at her home.

Mrs. Phifer kept open house during the war, and was active in every work for the Confederacy, many notables being entertained in her beautiful home.

Mrs. William White, of Charlotte, not only gave her six sons for the Confederacy, but gave of herself and her means to the cause. She was hostess to President Jefferson Davis and his escorts during their stay in Charlotte, when they met to consult as to the best course to pursue on their way to South Carolina. The home of Mrs. White is also one of the notable sights of the "Queen City."

Charlotte, being away from the seat of war and not in the path of invaders, did not bear the brunt of the Yankee army as did most of the larger towns farther east or south. However, two military companies, the Hornet's Nest and the Grays, kept the girls in a state of excitement with preparations for joining the Bethel regiment. The cadets of Col. D. H. Hill's Military Institute at Charlotte were busy drilling recruits from the adjoining counties, and the Sixth Regiment was encamped there. So the women had their time and thoughts full in work for the soldiers. Charlotte was considered a safe place from the Yankees, so constantly people from all over the lower part of North Carolina and South Carolina began to flock there as a haven of refuge. This gave added duties for the women of this fine community.

One of the splendid women of Charlotte was Mrs. Robert Burwell (Margaret Robertson), who not only gave her six sons to the Confederacy but performed a most important work, that of keeping her boarding school open (the Charlotte Female Institute) through the entire four years of the war. In addition to her large houseful of pupils Mrs. Burwell extended her limits to their utmost capacity to receive the girl refugees who sought safety from an invading army. Her sympathetic nature welcomed the strangers, and many still recall with gratitude the peaceful haven they found in her home. With all her duties in her school, Mrs. Burwell found time to minister to the needy families of soldiers and to work for the soldiers in the army. As a teacher this woman of the Sixties ranked high, and the part she took in keeping up the standard of education in the period of war deserves to be remembered, for her influence on every student left its mark toward the betterment of the State.

This Spartan mother, when two of her sons gave up their lives, illustrated "how sublime a thing it is to suffer and be strong," and renewed her services for others.

The aid society of Wadesboro was composed of some of North Carolina's most ardent women of the Confederacy, with Mrs. Jesse Edwards as president and Miss Kate Shepherd (afterwards the wife of Col. Risden Tyler Bennett), secretary. They and the other members went all over Anson County soliciting wool for knitting. They also gave magic lantern shows for funds for the society, going from town to town. When Sherman's army passed through Wadesboro these women exhibited the courage that characterized all of our North Carolina women. The wife of Bishop Atkinson, who was refugeeing there tied her husband's boots inside her hoop skirt and thus saved them for him. Miss Fan Beverly grabbed a freshly boiled ham and held it tightly during the Yankee raid. Mrs. Bennett in her exasperation extinguished a blaze started on their fine old sideboard, while at the Richardson home one of the daughters tied her brother's Masonic apron in front of his clothes and managed to save much.

The women of Louisburg and Franklin County were not behind the other women of North Carolina in real patriotism and self-sacrifice, for they gave freely of their heart's dearest treasures. They gave more soldiers to the Confederacy than there were voters in the county, eleven full companies. Through the Soldier's Aid Society the women of Louisburg never flagged in their service for their boys in gray, working early and late.

Judge Francis Winston, of Windsor, recalls an incident of the women's work in Franklin County, and the part he took in it as a small boy:

"I remember during the war the constant sewing and knitting that my mother (Mrs. Patrick Winston) had carried on and did herself in Franklin County, where we refugeed, and the articles were sent from there to the front. It's a pleasant memory to recall that I was very anxious to send a box of pop-corn to my uncle after the battle of Gettysburg, and how earnestly my mother undertook to dissuade me from doing so, but she finally yielded to my importunities and the large box of pop-corn, more than a bushel, was sent. You can imagine my great joy upon receipt of a letter from my uncle telling my mother that 'Frank's pop-corn came in fine shape and good time. My men had been without food for a day and a half and the pop-corn was all they had for another day. I doubt if such another scene was ever witnessed in any war as that night when Company C. and others of the regiment were busy around the fire light popping and eating this corn.'"

Louisburg has the honor of claiming the woman who made the first Stars and Bars flag, which was designed by Orren R. Smith. She was Mrs. Rebecca Winborne, whom the Division has remembered with a monument on which is carved the "Stars and Bars" of the Confederacy.

"There's a place in my heart for the stainless gray, for the Flag of the Stars and Bars."

BLOCKADE RUNNING INTO WILMINGTON

The Chase of the Blockade Runner

Freed from the lingering chase, in devious ways
    Upon the swelling tides
    Swiftly the Lilian glides
Through hostile shells and eager foeman past;
The lynx-eyed pilot gazing through the haze,
And engines straining, "far hope dawns at last."

Now falls in billows deep the welcome night
    Upon white sands below;
    While signal lamps aglow
Seek out Fort Fisher's distant answering gleams,
The blockade runner's keen, supreme delight—
Dear Dixie Land, the haven of our dreams!
    —Dr. James Sprunt, Wilmington, N.C.

There were many thrilling incidents during the war when the women of North Carolina proved themselves real heroines. One of these was Mrs. Louis H. DeRosset of Wilmington, a brave and charming woman. She with her infant daughter Gabrielle, were passengers on the noted blockade runner *Lynx*, which was commanded by Capt. Reed [Reid], one of the most daring spirits of the service. On the evening of September 16th, [the ship] attempted to run the blockade at New Inlet. She was immediately discovered by the Federal cruiser

Niphon, which fired several broadsides at her, nearly every shot striking the hull and seriously disabling her. Capt. [Reid] was almost escaping his pursuers, notwithstanding all this, but was again intercepted by the Federal men of war. Mrs. DeRosset and baby were put in the wheel house for safety, but here they were exposed to great danger, cannon balls passing close by them, so our heroine flew to the cabin with her baby.

As the vessel commenced sinking, Capt. [Reid], concerned for his passengers, headed for the beach. The sea was very rough that night and the treacherous breakers, with their deafening roar, afforded little hope of landing a woman and a baby through the surf; nevertheless it was the only alternative, and right bravely did this heroine meet it. Through the breakers the *Lynx* was driven to her destination. Boats were lowered with great difficulty, the sea dashing over the bulwarks and drenching sailors to the point of strangulation.

Mrs. DeRosset, with the utmost coolness, watched her chance, while the boat lurched and pounded against the stranded ship, and jumped to her place. The baby, wrapped in a blanket, was tossed from the deck to her mother ten feet below. And then the fight for a landing began. The whole crew, forgetful of their own danger, and inspired with courage by this brave lady's example, joined in three hearty cheers as she disappeared with her baby in the darkness toward shore.

Under the glare of the burning ship, a safe landing was made, but with great suffering. Soaking wet, without food or drink, they remained on the beach until an ambulance from Fort Fisher was sent to carry them twenty miles up to Wilmington.

The baby blockade runner (little Gabrielle) is now the charming Mrs. A. M. Waddell, president of the North Carolina Society, Colonial Dames. So she, and her brave mother, deserve to have their names recorded among North Carolina's heroic women of the Sixties.

Mrs. Josiah (Laura) Pender, of Tarboro, was another young woman who exhibited remarkable courage in running the blockade. She was returning from Bermuda to Wilmington on the ship of which her husband was captain, when a Federal gunboat fired upon the little blockade runner. The commander was on the point of surrendering, seeing the unequal fight, but the young wife declared that she would go out on deck and expose herself to the shot and shell if he surrendered. It is needless to say Capt. Pender surrendered to his wife and not to the Yankee commander. The Confederate runner made its port, and its valuable cargo for the Confederacy was saved through the courageous act of this young woman.

Mrs. Greenhow, Celebrated Spy

"And for those that lament them there is this relief,
That glory sits by the side of grief."

Though [she was] not a North Carolina woman by birth, yet the story of Mrs. Rose [O'Neal] Greenhow, the noted Confederate spy, of Washington City, is so closely linked with this State that we place her on the honor roll of our heroic women of North Carolina.

Mrs. Greenhow was a celebrated beauty, who rendered valuable service for the Confederacy in secret service work, receiving highest praise from the Confederate government. The ingenuity shown and the daring of this clever and courageous woman in getting through the lines important dispatches make one of the most interesting chapters in the story of the Confederacy. After serving so bravely Mrs. Greenhow was finally arrested and imprisoned in Washington City with her little girl, who showed the spirit of her mother when she told the officer in charge, "You have got here one of the worst little rebels you ever saw." Through much difficulty Mrs. Greenhow was released on account of the extreme illness of her daughter, and she again began her secret service work. On the night of September 30th, 1864, the blockade runner *Condor*, on which she was a passenger, arrived at the mouth of the Cape Fear River, trying to reach the port of Wilmington. Seeing that they were to be attacked by a Federal gunboat, Mrs. Greenhow asked to be put ashore in a small boat, for she had hidden on her person important papers for President Jefferson Davis, and she knew the danger of capture. As fate would have it, the little boat capsized and Rose Greenhow went to her death, for around her body was much gold that weighted her down. The next day her body was washed ashore. She was buried by the women of Wilmington, with the Confederate flag wrapped around her casket, in Oakwood [i.e., Oakdale] Cemetery. The important messages that she was guarding with her life were sent on to President Davis.

The grave of this beautiful heroine has been marked with a marble cross by the Ladies Memorial Association of Wilmington, and the name of Rose Greenhow will ever be remembered in North Carolina.

WOMEN IN NURSING AND HOSPITAL WORK

*"When pain and anguish wring the brow,
A ministering angel thou!"*

One of the brave self-sacrificing women of North Carolina who gave her services in nursing the sick and wounded was Mrs. Jesse (Annie K.) Kyle.

Having suffered the agony of having her husband under fire at Morris Island (with the Immortal Six Hundred), she offered her services (without pay) as head nurse at the hospital in Fayetteville. Mrs. Kyle, though a frail woman on crutches, had the indomitable spirit of a lion, working untiringly from morning 'til night dressing wounds, nursing the sick, soothing and comforting the dying with holy prayers.

Mrs. Kyle has left a most graphic reminiscence of Fayetteville at this time, in which she says:

"They were bringing the wounded from Fort Fisher, Wilmington, and other points. We already had one hospital and were establishing another. I shall never forget the doctor's look of amazement when I applied for the situation. My reply was: 'Doctor, I don't want any pay, but I must have constant occupation or I will lose my mind.' I went every morning at nine o'clock and stayed until one, and I always went late in the afternoon to see that the wants of the patients were attended during the night. I always dressed all the wounds every morning, and I soon found that my grief and sorrow were forgotten in administering to the wants of the sick. Such patience and fortitude I have never seen. Not one murmur did I ever hear escape the lips. My Prayer Book was my constant companion. I carried it in my pocket and many poor soldiers have I soothed and comforted with holy prayers. One day as I entered the hospital I noticed a new face. I made my way to him as I was struck by his gray hair, and said: 'You are too old to be here.' He smiled and his answer was quite a rebuke: 'One never gets too old to fight for one's home and fireside. I had no sons, so I came myself.'

"Often there were soldiers desperately ill with fever and other diseases, so the Young Ladies' Seminary on Hay Street in Fayetteville was fitted up as a hospital where they could be cared for. The three floors were arranged to accommodate the patients who were brought in from the different localities, many of them sick, some convalescing from typhoid fever, and some wounded. Each ward or floor was presided over by four ladies who attended to their wants giving medicine, nourishment, etc., also reading to them, writing to their absent loved ones, and making them as comfortable as possible, the doctor generally dressing their wounds.

"The hospital became crowded so another was fitted up, and it soon became full of patients.

"Many of the younger women assisted the older ones in caring for the sick soldiers, daily carrying flowers and delicacies, singing, and cheering them with sunny smiles.

"This service of the women of the Confederacy made what amends were possible for the pitiful absence of anesthetics.

"After Sherman's memorable visit to Fayetteville, March 11, '65, a Marine Hospital on Green Street was established. The meals for the sick soldiers in the hospital were supplied by the different ladies of the town, who took turns in sending them, several ladies being a committee on each day. It was very difficult to get medicine for the hospitals—all that reached Fayetteville being brought in by the blockade runner *Advance*. Most of the medicine used was quinine, which was very precious, but some medicines were made from herbs gathered from the woods.

"On the eleventh of March, Sherman, with his hordes of depraved and lawless men, came upon us bringing sorrow and desolation. I can never forget the terrible scene on that memorable morning, with Gen. Wade Hampton commanding the Confederate forces.

"About nine o'clock they sent for me to go to the hospital, and the horrible scene I witnessed there I shall never forget. The wounded had been brought in from Longstreet's battle, where a portion of Hardee's men had had an engagement with Sherman's men. I stayed with them till just before daylight and did all I could to relieve their wants. Even then I did not hear a single murmur. Such fortitude has NO PARALLEL IN HISTORY.

"O! THE HORRORS OF THOSE DAYS! It is impossible to write or tell what we endured, and it will never be known until we stand before the Judgment Seat of God. After the fall of Harper's Ferry the families and workmen were removed to Fayetteville, in consequence of which a number of handsome dwellings were added to the Arsenal grounds. It was a lovely spot, and we justly felt proud of it. But Sherman's torch reduced it to ashes. Fayetteville suffered more than most towns, for we had five cotton factories in the town and one at Rockfish [20th-century Hope Mills] just a few miles away, and they were all burned to the ground, leaving hundreds of people without work or any means of getting bread. And as we had been robbed of all we had, of course, we could not help them. As soon as night came on we could see fires in every direction, as all the buildings in the country were burned. I can compare it with nothing but what I can imagine Hades would be if its awful doors were thrown open. But for the kindness of my servants I don't know what would have become of me. They were very faithful. One walked up and down the passage all night, and the other stayed on the back porch. Still I was afraid to close my eyes. But for my nurse we would not have had one mouthful to eat. She hid some things in her own room and in that way saved them.

"The Yankees went into homes that were beautiful, rolled elegant pianos into the yard with valuable furniture, china, cut glass, and everything that was dear to the heart, even old family portraits, and chopped them up with axes—rolled barrels of flour and molasses into the parlors, and poured out their contents on beautiful carpets—in many cases set fire to lovely homes and burned them to the ground, and even took some of our citizens and hung them until their life was near extinct, to force them to tell them where their money was hidden; when alas! they had none to hide.

"After Sherman left, our hospitals which had not been very full were filled to overflowing. They came in with various diseases and wounds innumerable, while typhoid fever also prevailed. Every lady in town who could gave up her time to nursing and caring for the dear brave boys. We gave them medicine and took them flowers and wrote letters to their dear ones, who were far away from them, read to them, and did every thing possible to cheer and help them. Oh! how sad it was to see them suffer, and pass away so far from those they loved—and during their illness how they watched and waited day after day, for the letters from home that never came.

"One morning I had a message from the upper hospital

asking me to come. I got there in time to close the eyes of seven soldiers, then I went to the mayor and got a permit for a coffin and a hearse, then Mrs. Guion and I with two of the men from the hospital followed their remains to the place where we had been burying the soldiers.

"Just a few days after Sherman's army crossed the Cape Fear River I went to a few of my gentlemen friends and raised sufficient money to buy coffins and to have thirty graves dug. I had the six bodies in the hospital yard and the others buried where they camped disinterred, making twelve in all. Mayor McLean went to the cemetery with me to select a spot where we could have them all buried together. We could not get a square large enough to hold them all, so he gave us the back part of the cemetery, overlooking Cross Creek, a very pretty situation with room for all, and a place large enough left to place the monument. Eighteen were buried in a field across the creek and we had them all taken up, and just at sunset Dr. Huske, beloved rector of St. John's Church, read again the words: "I am the resurrection and the life," the coffins were lowered to their resting place, and the souls of the dead entered into the rest of Paradise until they should arise to meet the Lord and Savior."

The Women at Our State Capital

"Whose courage unbroken, whose sorrow unspoken,
Thrilled a cheer and a hope to the boys in gray."

The women of Raleigh, from the very beginning of the war, when the North Carolina soldiers were encamped there for training, had greater opportunity for service to our boys than any other town in the State. When Dr. Charles Johnston, head of the State Medical Department, called for volunteers among the women to nurse in the North Carolina hospitals in Petersburg, Va., a Raleigh woman, Miss M. L. Pettigrew, was among the three women chosen for this great service.

A wayside hospital was established here, and later other hospitals were opened and were constantly filled with soldiers brought here from many points. The Pettigrew hospital was where is now the State Soldiers' Home. The old Guion hotel and the churches were filled with the wounded, the unfinished building of Peace Institute was turned into a hospital, and many of the private homes were used to care for these men brought in on every train. How these women rescued their dead soldiers who were thrown in a field by the Yankees and began their Memorial Association is told further on in this chronicle.

The women of Raleigh endured the terror of Sherman's soldiers when they captured the State Capitol, and the days of reconstruction are very vivid today to those survivors of that period.

Capt. S. A. Ashe, in his history, says: "One of the Raleigh ladies in writing of the conditions in that city at this time gives these facts:

"Raleigh was now filled with wounded and disabled soldiers; the churches and every available place were turned into hospitals. I did what I could, but it seemed nothing; many poor men [lay] on benches, some in high delirium, some in the agony of death. A young soldier passed away; none knew his name or his home; as the coffin lid was being screwed down a dear old lady pressed her lips to his brow and said, 'Let me kiss him for his dear old mother.' Every heart responded and all eyes were filled with tears. Volumes of heart-rending and pathetic incidents of our four years' cruel war. Although we were becoming less hopeful, yet the fall of the Confederacy was unexpected at last."

"Is it your prayer that the world may know
The knightly deeds of the stainless dead?"

Mrs. Martha Haywood gives these sacred recollections of the Confederate days in Raleigh.

"My most vivid recollections of the war in Raleigh are closely related to Christ Church, there we used to go for the strength and inspiration to carry us through the dark days that were upon us. To listen to the council of our pastor Doctor Mason. To pray for the Confederate government and its leader, Jefferson Davis. There is an old legend that the golden cock on the steeple of Christ Church is the only article resembling a fowl that Sherman's bummers did not take when they passed through our city. Great would have been the grief of our congregation had the steeple been low enough to permit their trying their hand at its capture, for day by day it had spoken to us of hope, reminding us that each day was a new day, calling on us to hold to the faith, no matter how hard the winter of discontent. Never to deny by word or action our belief in the goodness of God—our faith in our Redeemer. Around the church clustered our strength and our hope for the Life Eternal—here the men and boys who had left us to fight for the right, came sometimes back on their furloughs to join their prayers with ours—here their sweethearts, wives, and mothers came to pray for their safety during the long cold days of dread. The dim, quiet aisles are always peopled for me with pretty brides of those days—the sad-faced widows. Here in the quiet light I catch again the ghostly glimmer of Generals Branch and Cox, here the voices of the choir in the old hymns of faith and courage. We offered the bell of the church to the Confederate government, but it was never removed, for into each heart had crept the knowledge that all we could do was too little to stem the mighty tide that was upon us.

The voice of the old bell speaks ever to my heart, of the golden days before the cruel war, the gray days when our faith rose triumphant in prayers and hymns.

"No country or clime hath devotion like thine."

Among the many women of our State whose ministrations to the soldiers of the Confederacy should be recorded is Mrs. Sarah E. Elliott. Mrs. Elliott refugeed from her home in Elizabeth City to Oxford during the war, and while in the latter town she gave special work in nursing at the hospital at Kittrell Springs. This was one of the fashionable watering places in antebellum days and had been converted into a hospital by the Confederate government, to which were sent hundreds of sick and wounded soldiers.

Mrs. Elliott and other ladies of this section were the ministering angels at this hospital. She not only sent wagons loaded with delicacies and food from the opening of it until the last, but spared no pains to induce others to do the same. She tenderly nursed these soldiers and was untiring in her efforts to relieve their suffering. Over fifty of these patients of the Kittrell Springs hospital died and were buried near the town of Kittrell. Mrs. Elliott in 1871 rescued these graves from oblivion and with her own hands planted a cedar hedge around the plot, fencing it in and making it one of the loveliest of God's acres in the State.

A tribute should be paid to Mrs. John Harper, whose colonial house stood near the sight of the battle of Bentonville (March 19, '65), not far from Goldsboro. This dauntless woman went forth upon this scene of carnage and battle, and with the aid of her children, gathered into her home the wounded, whom she nursed as best she could, bathing the fevered brow and sending the departed souls on wings of prayer to God. Then she gave burial to these, and to those who were left on the field of battle in the dire calamity that pressed the Confederate forces.

"All hail to you, Sisters of warm blooded skies,
Proud mothers of chivalrous men."

Amongst the Florence Nightingales of North Carolina were the women of the Farquhard [Smith], William [Smith], and John Smith families of the Little River community in Harnett (then Cumberland) County. The battle of Averasboro, between Sherman's army and Johnston's, was fought on March 16th, 1865, in the beautiful grove of Mr. John Smith. Instead of flying from this terrifying scene, the women of this family assisted in carrying the wounded and dying into this home, and turned the entire house into a hospital. The men were tenderly and lovingly nursed by the older women while the young ladies of the family and the community brought every delicacy that could be concocted from their meager supplies (after Sherman's destruction). The main line of battle extended through the section where Chicora Cemetery now stands. The breastworks, part of which still remain, extended from Black River across to the Cape Fear River, a distance of several miles.

Miss Jessie Slocumb Smith, granddaughter of Mrs. Farquhard Smith, one of the Florence Nightingales of the battle of Averasboro, gives this description of the homes of the three "mothers," who bore such important parts in this event of the war.

"During the battle of Averasboro the home of Mrs. Farquhard Smith was confiscated by the Federal troops and used as their headquarters. The William Smith home, now standing just as in the Sixties, was used as a Federal hospital. The 'parlor' on which the blood stains are yet to be seen was used as an operating room, and the piano, now the treasured possession of a granddaughter, was used for an operating table. The Federal soldiers dying here were first buried in the garden, but all of these, as well as those killed in the battle of Averasboro, were later moved to the Federal cemetery in Raleigh.

"The most interesting of the three homes is the old John Smith place, Oak Grove, which was vacated by the families and used as the Confederate hospital. It is one of the few homes to which the passing years has brought no architectural changes. It still stands, though now more than a century old, as simply and as proudly as in those trying days of '65! In the attic are still to be seen the holes made by the cannonballs, and on an upstairs bedroom floor are still discernible the blood stains left by wounded Confederate soldiers. To this hospital most of the wounded were carried—all who could be accommodated. When, however, its rooms were filled to overflowing, other homes and neighbors came to the rescue.

"After fighting all day our men were compelled to withdraw with great loss of life. Those who escaped were so closely pressed that they were unable to bury their dead, so the enemy placed the bodies in hastily dug graves.

"As interesting as the battlefield are the homes of the neighborhood, Smithville it was called. These homes escaped the torch usually applied because, I suppose, they were necessary to the Union troops. The Farquhard Smith home was used as headquarters for the Federal troops.

"Only those who have heard the women of that day talk realize the poverty of those days for this community. First Johnston's army had passed through, taking the necessary supplies for our men, and then came Sherman's army, pillaging everything. For food there was only a little corn left, and sometimes some meat which had been buried or hidden. Great was the problem of procuring food for the patients at the hospital. The ladies living near by, who went in to nursing each day, carried part of their frugal supper of corn muffin and hominy, while those living farther away, those who had saved some cows and chickens and so had milk and eggs, made such delicacies as they could contrive and sent each day to the hospital.

"We of the present day can but marvel that there was sufficient strength and spirit left after going through all the hardships of that period for the women to begin immediately the work of 'carrying on!' However they did it."

ARRIVAL OF A FORAGING PARTY.

A FORAGING PARTY

Drawn by one of Sherman's soldiers, and copied by the author from a magazine of the Sixties. This illustrates many of the incidents we are recording, where homes were ruthlessly pillaged. [The art above is reproduced from the original engraving.]

COURAGE DISPLAYED

"Let Evil come with angry brow, a lionhearted hero thou."

In one of the issues of that valuable magazine, *Carolina and the Southern Cross*, Mrs. [Lillie] Archbell gives this thrilling story of a young girl in Kinston (who was later Mrs. Minnie Suggs). After telling of the indignities and desperations of the Yankees in Kinston, Mrs. Suggs says: "As I looked from the window of my home I saw those brutal Yankees hang my little brother (in a kind of gallows used to swing hogs) and calling my mother, I rushed from the house like fury. I no longer knew what fear was. I seized the collar of the Yankee who was drawing the child up the gallows and shook him until he released the rope. By that time Mother came and helped unhang the boy, who was as white as a sheet and shaking with ague. Mother put him to bed, and those Yankees left."

This same girl again showed the splendid courage of so many of our Confederate women. One day when she was alone in her country home with only her cook, a Yankee and a negro rode up. The Yankee called to the negro to come in and help him burn the house. In telling the story Mrs. Suggs says: "'No,' I said, stepping on the porch. 'That negro knows better than to come in. If he comes in I shall kill him.' I saw that the negro did not offer to come, but the white man began to move the chairs into the center of the room and called to our cook to bring fire. She refused, but he kept moving things and calling for fire. In order to move a table he placed his gun by the door. I saw my advantage, and reached it just as he realized what I was doing. I did not have time to aim the gun but I raised it like a club and told him that I would use it if he came near me. The negro on horseback rode off as soon as he saw me with the gun.

"'Hold up your hands,' I said to the Yankee, and his hands went up. 'Now,' I said, 'Go and get on your horse.' He did so, but he begged me to let him have the gun. He said he would have to tell what had become of it. The rifle contained fifteen leads. I looked at the Yankee and told him that I would return the gun if he would take an oath. He agreed. 'Raise your right hand,' I said, 'and repeat the oath after me: I swear before Almighty God that I will go home and never fire another gun at a Southerner.' He raised the hand and took the oath; I handed him the gun. Somehow I felt safe in doing so. He took off his cap and said: 'You brave girl. No man could harm you after such a daring act, and I wish for you only what is good,' and he rode away."

The variety of war industries carried on in Kinston was very great, and the women did a large part of the work. There were three hospitals in which the women nursed, besides a long line of tents used for smallpox cases.

"Aunt Abby, the Irrepressible"

"What could daunt her, what could turn her?"

Mrs. Abby House of Franklin County, made famous from Mrs. Mary Bayard Clarke's sketches as "Aunt Abby, the Irrepressible," though a "diamond in the rough" was one of the strangest and most courageous characters among our women of the Sixties. Unable to read or write, she could use her tongue most effectively, as on her frequent visits to Gen. Lee, President Davis, and Governor Vance, when she showed her determination by always gaining her point in her efforts to obtain furloughs for sick soldiers. Mrs. Clarke quotes her as saying to her eight nephews, "I can tell you not a man of my family would I let stay at home in peace if he was able to tote a musket. I said to them, boys, all 'er you go along to the field whar you belongs, and if any of you gits sick or is wounded, you can depend on your old aunt Abby to nuss and tend you. For so help me God if one of you gits down and I can't git to you no other way, I'll foot it to your bedside; and if anyone of you dies or gits killed, I promise to bring you home and bury you with your kin."

Faithfully did she keep her promise, as five of the eight sleep in soldier's graves, nursed, or his body brought home by this fearless woman; even for twelve days searching the battlefields, herself unmindful of its horrors, and walking, even running, to Richmond to nurse her boys. "Aunt Abby" was as fearless under fire as in the use of her tongue, and with the greatest coolness, she would walk through the trenches during the fearful bombardment of Petersburg, frequently going under heavy fire to carry water to our wounded. On one occasion finding two horses whose riders had jumped off to run down some Yankees, she carefully led them by the bridle to find their owners with the bullets around her like hail, and she as cool as though leading the horses to water at home.

She was on the way to Gen. Lee's army when she heard of the evacuation of Richmond and President Davis's arrival at Greensboro, so she "footed" it down the railroad track to join her beloved Davis since she couldn't "git to Gen'ral Lee."

Reaching Greensboro she says she "cooked the last mouthful o' vittles Jeff Davis eat in North Carolina, and he shuck hands with me when the train started, and said, 'Good-bye Aunt Abby, you are true grit, and stick to your friends to the last, but's no more than I thought you'd do.'"

Her fearlessness in forcing the Federal Provost Marshal at Raleigh to give her back her mule, "crap critter," as she called it, which Sherman's "bummers" had stolen, fully carried out Governor Vance's description of this unique character in a letter to Gen. Lee as "The ubiquitous, indefatigable and irrepressible Mrs. Abby Horne House."

Other Heroines

> "No army's private soldiers ever may
> Have quite so many tributes; they shall be
> Forever held in memory with Lee,
> Remembered, loved, forever and a day!"

Gen. William A. Smith, commander of the North Carolina Division, United Confederate Veterans, gives this thrilling story of a heroine of Sherman's raid in Anson County.

"When the Federal army commanded by Gen. Sherman passed through the southern portion of Anson County, January and February 1865, occupying a week in passing, the L. D. Bennett home lay in his track. [Sherman's] soldiers set fire to the gin house and burned more than two hundred bales of cotton, the corn crib and contents, and the granary with its wheat, oats, and field peas; robbed the smokehouse; and destroyed every thing that would sustain life. The way to conquer the South was to conquer the women of the South—the sustainers of the army in the field—the only way to conquer the Southern women was to starve them and their children. In this they reckoned without their host, as the Southern women were unconquerable.

> "No annals of the world has ever told
> Of grander, more unselfish sacrifice,
> More loyal hearts in God's paradise
> And sacred scribe has never yet unrolled."

"[The soldiers] hooked up two magnificent bays to the finest carriage in Anson County and loaded it with hams from the smokehouse and drove away—it was never seen more. They drove off or wantonly shot every horse and mule, every cow and calf. Flocks of sheep and goats did not escape. Killed the peafowls, the ducks, guineas, and chickens. The only feathered thing that escaped was a gander. For three or four days during the passing of Sherman's army, he [Bennett] was without food or water. Afterward he came out of hiding. The Bennett family kept it [the gander] as [a] relic till it became so old that a breadcrust, when given was carried by him to the chicken trough and soaked—softened so he could eat it.

"They carried off the watches and jewelry and silverware, not leaving so much as a teaspoon. Broke into and ransacked the trunks, bureaus, and closets. The piano, sofas, dining table, bureaus, and other large furniture [were] cut up into fragments with an axe. They did not spare the old walnut and mahogany bedsteads. Opened the ticks and scattered the feathers over the floors of the chambers; with buckets brought molasses (sorghum) and mixed it with the feathers by thoroughly stirring.

"The five sons of the Bennett family were all in the Confederate army. Mrs. Jane Bennett and two daughters, Mary and Charlotte, were the only occupants of the dwelling. When the Yankees came the mother and daughters retired into one room, locked the door, and gave up the other portion of the house. After [the Yankees] had destroyed everything, (took what they desired and tore up the balance), and wrought their fiendish will in both stories and attic, the vandals approached the door of the room where the mother and maiden daughters were. This they found locked and were preparing to break the door down. Then it was thrown open by the elder maiden with a repeating gun in her hand. Said she, 'I will kill the first man who enters.' They looked at the repeating gun, then along its shining barrel saw the scintillating beads of determination in the flashing eyes of the heroic girl, and steady hands of the resolute girl behind the gun, and dared not enter. Thus she saved her honor and protected her mother and sister.

"A man would not be brave enough to resist a horde of determined men bent on mischief, pillage, and vandalism, but Miss Mary Bennett dared to and did defy them. Seeing an officer in their midst she asked him for a guard to be stationed at the door, which was done.

"The above story and incident is literally true as heard from the lips of Miss Bennett, for I married this HEROINE."

Capt. Ashe tells us of how venerable Bishop Thomas Atkinson, at his home at Wadesboro on March 3, 1865, was insulted by Sherman's soldiers. Bishop Atkinson said, "When the Yankees entered the town I requested my family to remain in their rooms. A soldier entering the door with many oaths demanded my watch which I refused to give up. He then presented a pistol at me, and threatened to shoot me if I did not surrender it immediately. I still refused, and the altercation became loud and my wife heard it and ran into the room and beseeched me to give it up, which I then did. He then proceeded to rifle our trunks and drawers, and took some of my clothes from these and my wife's jewelry."

*"What will not woman, gentle woman dare,
When strong affection stirs her spirit up?"*

When Sherman's army was passing through Clinton, Sampson County, some of the soldiers attacked the home of Robert A. Moseley, commander of the Home Guard, who had been forced on account of illness to return home from active duty. It was during the night that the Yankee soldiers entered the home. They pulled open the trunks and drawers in search of valuables, then threw a large feather pillow on the infant Robert Moseley, Jr., who lay asleep on his mother's bed. Like an enraged tigress Mrs. Moseley sprang up in defense of her baby, exclaiming, "Would you murder a helpless child?" With an oath the ruffian said, "The d____ little rebel ought to be smothered." Just then a scream of "Brother, brother," was heard, and Robert Moseley rushed to the room occupied by his wife's eighteen-year-old sister, which had been entered by the marauders. After plundering the bedroom and terrifying the young girl and her two little sisters, Anna and Ida, the soldiers left with curses and threats.

This incident was given me by Mrs. Moseley herself, now a lovely and cultured old lady in her nineties. Her delicate soldier husband passed to the Beyond soon after Sherman's soldiers attacked his home, leaving her (who had been raised in wealth) to face the poverty of reconstruction days with five small children. How this young woman showed pluck and heroism in raising and educating these as splendid men and women is another story. But the spirit was characteristic of our Southern women of the Sixties.

As Mrs. Mary A. Corbett, of Ivanhoe, Sampson County, lay in bed with a two-day-old infant, Sherman's soldiers, trying to terrify her into disclosing her hidden valuables, started a fire beneath her bedroom window, the flames mounting high. In order to save her fatherless babes, she gave the information.

A thrilling act of courage was exhibited by Mrs. Henry Finch, of Johnston County. In retaliation for Wheeler's Calvary cutting off part of Sherman's army train, the Yankee soldiers locked Mrs. Finch inside her home and set fire to the building. This intrepid woman raised the window, jumped to the ground, pointed a gun, and threatened to shoot, saying she preferred to be shot by them than burned to death. The soldiers admired her courage allowed her to walk over to the adjoining plantation. The home of Mrs. Lucien Saunders in Johnston County was also destroyed, and through it all Mrs. Saunders showed this same splendid spirit which characterized our Southern women.

Mrs. Evelyn Smith Beckwith, while refugeeing from Craven County at Smithfield, Johnston County, had a terrible experience with Sherman's soldiers. With no one in the house but herself and four small children, negro troops, commanded by white men, came upon them and demanded hidden silver. One of the officers threatened to hang Mrs. Beckwith and the children, and burnt her home, finally saying, "Madam, do you know we sometimes divest the Southern women of their clothes?" This indauntable woman replied that she was not afraid of him, and that if he dared deprive her of her clothes he would never get on his horse again. And these ruffians departed overcome by her superb fearlessness.

The same fearlessness was shown by Mrs. Murdock White, a young woman of Sampson County. When part of Sherman's army was engaged in their destructive visit to Sampson County they came upon her house. With a pistol placed at the head of Mrs. White they demanded the hidden valuables. This courageous woman said, "Shoot, I'll never tell you where they are"—whereupon the ruffians departed from the house disgusted.

Miss Nellie Worth (now Mrs. George French, of Wilmington), when Sherman's army were devastating eastern Carolina, had a Yankee present a pistol at her head and threatened to kill her if she didn't tell where the valuables were hidden. This courageous young girl, though completely in his power, defied and dared him to touch her, refusing to give the desired information. Finding his threats were useless, the disgusted "bummer" left swearing, as Miss Worth expressed it, "I was 'the d——st rebel he had ever seen' (which I considered quite a compliment)."

The experience of Mrs. Rachael Foy, the widow of Enoch Foy, who lived near New Bern, was very harrowing. Her only son, Franklin, was a scout in very hazardous service for the army, a reward being offered by the Federals for his capture. As Foy was "scouting" in the district around New Bern bringing in valuable information, the Yankees, thinking he would visit his mother and his small children (who lived in that vicinity), came out from New Bern eight hundred strong. In their efforts to capture Foy, they surrounded Mrs. Rachael Foy's home, locking her and her grandchildren in a room, giving all her keys to the slaves, making them rulers over her household. They camped in her grove for three days, not allowing anything to be carried to her, though some of her faithful servants secretly slipped food and water. Finally the soldiers marched off without capturing the scout Foy. In the home of Mrs. Gillette they encountered Confederate soldiers, and a skirmish took place in the large grove of this home. Mrs. Gillette was very ill and not able to be moved to a place of safety. In the excitement she rolled off her bed, a bullet *passing through the bed where she had been lying!*

The story of how a young girl of twelve years cleverly outwitted a Yankee officer shows that even the children were on the alert to help their Southland.

The home of Mrs. Robert Roundtree, near Kinston, was invaded by the Federal soldiers and pillaged. The officer in charge made the young daughter, Rose (a beautiful girl of twelve) sit at the piano and play for him. After this he forced her to accompany him on a drive, while the frantic mother, unprotected, could only plead for her child in vain. This girl, though young in years, sensed her danger, and as she and her captor drove past a thick wood she exclaimed, "There's where my brother has his company of Confederate soldiers." Her ruse worked well, for the Yankee officer immediately wheeled, threw the girl from the vehicle, and dashed madly down the road. After this it was observed that the Federals who had been hanging around the vicinity, all disappeared, evidently believing that our soldiers were secreted there. This girl was afterwards Mrs. William Kennedy, of Kinston, an accomplished musician and beauty of the Sixties.

The story of the services of beautiful Daisy Chaffee, wife of Col. William Lamb, commander of Fort Fisher (until wounded), stands out as one of the brightest chapters of the history of the women in North Carolina in the Confederacy. While [she was] not a North Carolina woman, this State claimed her from 1863 until the end of the war in '65. Declining the use of several spacious homes near Wilmington, Mrs.

Lamb took up her abode in a three-room log house at Fort Fisher, in order to be near her devoted husband (to sustain and cheer him), being the only white woman living in this vicinity. This young woman gained the titles of "Heroine of Fort Fisher," and "Angel of the Fort," by serving the sick and wounded soldiers and sailors there, under conditions that would have tried the soul of most women. Her bravery was fully shown during the terrific bombardment of Fort Fisher, and her faith was sustained through it all. It was Mrs. Lamb who helped to tenderly prepare for burial the body of Rose Greenhow, the celebrated Confederate spy, who was drowned off Fort Fisher. The full and thrilling story of Mrs. Lamb has been recently given by Louis T. Moore, a talented historian of Wilmington.

CANTEEN WORK

---

*"The scene shall fade from my memory never,
For Dixie Land, hooray forever."*

Little bands of women canteen workers in all our principal towns along the railroad met trains bearing the wounded, often in the darkness of night, with such refreshments as they could provide, and often clothed, fed, and comforted these weary men. News from home and camp was eagerly exchanged before the train departed.

Mrs. J. Henry Smith, of Greensboro, tells of the memorable night of the battle of Bentonville, March 19, '65, when the war in its stern and startling reality came to their very door. Without warning or preparation, the wounded were brought to Greensboro in such numbers as to fill the churches, court house, and every available space in the town, where beds were hastily improvised. To that clarion call the women of Greensboro responded with one accord. With tender hearts and eager hands they nursed, and out of their scanty food these women fed, these dear soldiers, each neighborhood feeding from their own tables the body of soldiers nearest them. Soon after the ill and wounded were transported to the historic mansion of Edgeworth Seminary, which was used as a hospital.

Many interesting incidents connected with the women of Greensboro have been preserved through a "reminiscence" of Mrs. Lettie Walker, a daughter of Gov. James L. Morehead, one of North Carolina's most distinguished sons. Other incidents of Greensboro have been given in previous articles, and these may be added to the history of Guilford County's women of the Sixties. Mrs. James Morehead had the honor of being hostess to Gen. Beauregard and staff, in March 1865, at her mansion Bland Wood. President and Mrs. Davis remained over one night in Greensboro, declining Gov. and Mrs. Morehead's invitation "lest the Federal troops should burn the house that sheltered him for one night." Members of the Confederate Cabinet Alexander Stephens and Gen. Joseph E. Johnston were guests of the Moreheads after Lee's surrender, as they journeyed from Richmond, also Gen. Lee's brother, who commanded army stores sent from Richmond. The Federal generals Burnside, Schofield, and Kilpatrick with their staffs sent word to the mayor that they would occupy the largest house in town, so they came to Bland Wood, which already held three families and many sick soldiers. The story has been told before of how Greensboro women met the trains bearing the wounded and dying, seeing boxes filled with dead bodies piled high on the railroad platform, with dying soldiers lying near to be cared for. It was an awful experience through which Mrs. Walker and these brave women passed, but with loving care.

Mrs. M. L. Crutchfield, who is now in her eighties and a resident of the Masonic home at Greensboro, tells of the time when as Margaret Holt, a maiden of twenty years, she lived at Swepsonville and took part in feeding the army of soldiers of the Confederate army. She remembers with remarkable vividness the picture of that day in which the Confederate forces crossed Haw River.

Patriotic citizens here and there, along the sparsely settled banks of the river, were scraping together all the supplies that could be found in those Southern homes, which in the latter part of the conflict had in many instances bare cupboards. The soldiers were sick and hungry.

"It was in the fall of the year when the soldiers began to pass. They were hungry and some of them were half naked. Lots of them had no shoes and many of them fell down with all kinds of sickness."

Long into the night Margaret stood at her post heating edibles for the soldiers of her country. Things were getting low. Bread was given out without much gravy on it, and then from the cupboard the preserves were brought out, the preserves that had been made a few weeks before out of cane sorghum.

And still they came, barefoot soldiers, hungry soldiers, hatless soldiers, marching to no rhythmic drumbeat nor with no flying banner but just "a walking along" shuffling, some of the more fortunate ones riding horses that were nearly broken down. The crossing of the river was a slow process. It had to be forded over a raised bed that was just wide enough to accommodate one vehicle at a time.

For thirty-six hours, according to Mrs. Crutchfield, who was the girl at the oven, the forces were continuously filing across the river. Many of them never got across, but fell by the way with one of the terrible diseases so common to the army of the Sixties.

OTHER INCIDENTS OF WOMENS' WORK

"They, patient, fed the patriotic fires."

From the pen of Miss Georgia Hicks, of Faison (an ex-historian of this division), we have some interesting history of the war days in Duplin County.

"Our home on the Goldsboro and Wilmington road was the highway of the passage of Confederate troops to and fro. My mother, Mrs. Eliza Hicks, wife of Dr. James H. Hicks, was an ardent Confederate, and made much clothing for the soldiers from her plantation. She always had quantities of good food ready for our soldiers and would send it to the road gate for them as they passed, the officers coming to the house. Her home made one of the stations for couriers, who were stationed every ten miles, and carried messages, day and night. Mother reserved one room in the house for these Confederate Couriers. In March '65, the army of Generals Terry and Sherman came to Duplin County on their way to Raleigh, Terry coming from Fort Fisher and Sherman from South Carolina. I have heard mother say that Gen. Terry (whose headquarters were at the home of my sister, Mrs. C. D. Hill) was always kind and a thorough gentleman, as were the members of his staff, very different from Sherman and his officers. Mrs. Hill rendered real service to one of Terry's staff, who was desperately ill, in nursing him, and he attributed his recovery largely to her. The behavior of Sherman's army around Faison is but a repetition of the treatment of the people wherever they went.

"In the home of Mrs. Rachel Pearsal of Duplin County, her aunt, aged and ill, was thrown from her bed on the floor, so that they could look for valuables they thought hidden there.

"I was a school-girl at Saint Mary's in Raleigh and I will never forget the feeling of the girls, when Johnston's army passed by. The Federal Gen. Howard was encamped in Saint Mary's grove for weeks, and we were in a state of excitement all the time."

There were seven Hicks boys, of the Faison community, in the War between the States, and each played his part valiantly. They were Capt. Lewis, Dr. John, Lt. A. D., Elias, John, Lyde, and Albert.

A very thrilling escape from death by the Yankees was made by Dr. James H. Hicks, the father of Miss Georgia Hicks, the narrator of the above incidents. Sherman's army was encamped near the home of Mrs. James H. Hicks. This courageous woman with a sorrowful heart saw her husband, that splendid physician, carried away in the night by the soldiers on the pretext of attending a sick man. Mrs. Hicks pleaded with him not to go, but his one thought was to relieve suffering. He was carried far away, and when he was brought by hours later, he had the appearance of a man that had almost seen death. These ruffians hung this fine old gentleman up by the neck twice, in their endeavor to secure information as to hidden valuables. They finally released their victim, who refused to divulge his secrets. Dr. Hicks never recovered from this terrible shock and his wife never mentioned it, for she was almost prostrated over his treatment by these ruffians. In the same house lived Miss Rachael McIver, "sister cousin" of Mrs. Hicks, who said always that she never knew why, but she was never afraid of the Yankee soldiers. One day when a man came downstairs with his arms full of silk dresses, she ordered him to put them down. He laughed loud, jumped on his horse, and galloped away.

Though not in the direct path of the invaders, the old town of Pittsboro, Chatham County, was filled with women who refugeed there from the Cape Fear section. These assisted the Pittsboro women in making garments and knitted for the soldiers, their Aid Society being active in keeping the boys at the front supplied. Mrs. John Jackson (Lucy Worth) inherited some of the executive ability of her father, Jonathan Worth, Reconstruction governor and war treasurer of the State, and was one of the most inventive women of this community, showing remarkable skill in her work. She cut up her handsome carpets, as did many other Southern women, and devised many things to cheer these poor men. Her daughter, Bettie (Mrs. Henry A. [London]), has kept up her mother's enthusiasm in the Cause, and as a devoted member and former president of the North Carolina Division, United Daughters of the Confederacy, she has paid loving tribute to the men who followed Lee, and whose soldier-boy husband carried the last message at Appomattox, to "cease firing."

The young women of the London family in Pittsboro were among the active workers of this section and gave comfort to many a needy family of the men in the army. Miss Mary London (later Mrs. Josh T. James of Wilmington) showed the courageous spirit of many Southern girls when threatened by Sherman's bummers with a pistol at her head to disclose the family silver (this at a friend's in Wadesboro).

Old Salem was far removed from the seat of warfare, but the women of this Moravian community were very active in their work. Their Soldier's Aid society was early organized, and a description of her flag presentation is given further on in this story. The famous Female Academy of old Salem was kept open through the entire war and opened its doors, as did the one in Charlotte, to girls who were refugeeing from eastern Carolina.

Many older women found refuge in this hospitable town, from the seat of warfare. Occasionally bands of Yankee soldiers came through Forsyth County, and these Confederates did not escape being pillaged. They gave generously of their provisions to help feed Lee's army, and their soldiers fought valiantly in the field.

Splendid Services of a Kinston Woman

A woman of Kinston, a Northern woman by birth, but who married a Southern man in 1857, deserves to be remembered as one of our women of this State who bore an important part in the War between the States.

This was Mrs. Anderson Roscoe Miller (Dellia Maria Henry), the mother of Mrs. H. O. Hyatt, an honored member of the U.D.C. in Kinston. Being left at the very beginning of the war, her husband, Dr. Miller, volunteering at the first call of arms, this young woman was placed in a most difficult position. Being a Northern woman made both sides suspect that she was a spy, and she suffered many unjust persecutions. When the Northern troops first entered Kinston and were looting the town Mrs. Miller succeeded in securing from the

Federal general a guard for the whole town, explaining that she was the daughter of a leading Mason of Vermont. Her timely intervention prevented an attack on the young ladies of Kinston, whom the marauders were threatening. Mrs. Hyatt, the daughter of Mrs. Miller, in a most interesting story of her mother's experiences during the war, says:

"Kinston was a battleground twice during the war and was occupied frequently by both Southern and Northern troops. Whenever there were soldiers in the hospital my mother took or sent soups and other things to the hospital every day. Once when the town was evacuated hurriedly by the Southern troops she felt for three days she must still go to the hospital. On the third day she told her servant, Aunt Harriet, she could stand it no longer; she must go. When she arrived she found nine Southern soldiers, too sick to be removed, who had been without food or water for three days. She and Aunt Harriet bathed [them], dressed their wounds, and fed them.

"My mother went home to visit her parents in the summer of '61, taking me with her. I was taken with diphtheria, and at the same time she received a letter telling her not to attempt to return as the lines were practically closed. Her people tried to keep her but she would not stay. She said, 'I have cast my fortunes there and I must go.' She left me sick and the comforts of a safe home to take the place she felt duty called her to take. Most of the first families of the town who were able to do so refugeed to the western part of the State to avoid the terrors and depredations of war, and she was throughout the whole war in a position to defend and comfort those who did not refugee. She gave her whole heart to this service, and was a great help to many in desperate need.

"About the first of February in '65, she went to Vermont to bring me home. She carried tobacco beneath a false bottom in her trunk, which she sold in New York to help pay her expenses. Returning she filled the space with twenty-five dollars' worth of needles, which were long before this time very scarce in the South. Going, she drove through the country to New Bern by way of Trenton. Returning, at New Bern she found the largest force of Yankees that had ever been there. She tried for several days to get through the lines with me and almost despaired of doing so. Finally she met on the street, by accident, an old friend who was an officer in the Union army. She told him she was trying to get home. He said, 'Our orders are very strict. No one is to leave town until our next move is made.' She insisted that he take her to the commander anyway. This officer asked her if she would be willing to go up the river with the gunboats as a prisoner of war. She said, 'If it is God's will I shall live to get home with my child, if it is not I may as well die in one place as another.' She believed in a personal God and protecting angels. So she and I came up the river with gunboats that were throwing shells on the town. My mother begged the officer in charge of the boat to shoot up the river instead of at the town so as not to hurt the women and children, which he did, he said, for a brave woman. She had to clutch me tightly every time a gun was fired to keep me from jumping overboard. We landed after the battle near the old Graham place. The river bridge had been burned down by the Confederates to retard pursuit, and we had to cross the river on boats.

"My father came from the war ruined in health; his nerves were prostrated, and for two or three years he was so ill that he did not even wish to work. How my mother put her shoulder to the wheel, taking the small amount of life insurance left by her father and opening a millinery store in the parlor of her home, is a story of splendid determination of a woman. It was said she was the only person who went into business immediately after the war who did not go into bankruptcy. She was a skillful manager, but she was also a rigid economist when in debt. She believed in education, and even through the trying days of the war and reconstruction she found time to teach her children. She originated the movement for the first school in Kinston, subscribing the first twenty-five dollars. Though ill in health, she continued her work until it was completed, her determination and courage winning the admiration of all who knew her. Her brother William was on the train once and overheard some men discussing her. They said, 'She is the ablest woman in North Carolina.' Many persons who have had business dealings with her have said, 'She was the finest woman I have ever known.'

"She said, 'I have lived a thousand deaths: it is easy for me to die.'"

"O yes, I am a Southern girl, and I glory in the name."

Mrs. Ida Wilkins of Weldon, one of the oldest and most honored members of the North Carolina Division, United Daughters of the Confederacy, gives us glimpses of the Sixties, when she was a young girl. She says, "There were four companies known as Light Infantry at the beginning of the War between the States: one was from Fayetteville, one from Wilmington, one from Wilson, one from Halifax. In April 1861, the Halifax company were quartered in Weldon for quite a while being instructed at preparing for service. How handsome they appeared to my girlish eye in their gay uniforms and plumed hats. There was great anxiety as to which regiment they would be assigned to hoping they would be assigned to the first North Carolina regiment.

"The Enfield Blues, another old company from Halifax County, was the one assigned to the First Regiment, greatly to the disappointment of the Light Infantry boys.

"Those were troublous times, and the memory of them is still very vivid to me. The history of these four Light Infantry companies should live, and the fact that they were all organized companies prior to 1860 proves their service, which was further emphasized most valiantly in the Confederate army.

"The 'Hornet's Nest Rifles' of Charlotte also came through Weldon on the way to the front. The file leader carried on his bayonet a big hornet's nest, which attracted much attention.

"The women of Weldon gave loving service in nursing the wounded, as a wayside hospital was established here at the beginning of the war, Weldon being on the direct route of transportation. The Methodist church was used as a hospital, and the home of Mrs. Hamlin Allen was filled with the soldiers.

"Our women were active and untiring all through the war, and we young girls tried to assist the older ones in their work for the boys in gray."

Miss Annie Ellison of Coleraine, Bertie County, was one of the most active young women of that section in work for the soldiers. She traveled over her entire county on horseback alone, soliciting clothing for the needy soldiers. When her soldier sweetheart, Lt. Col. Thomas Sharp, returned home after the war he found that this lovely young girl had been called to the Beyond.

Mrs. John Mercer, of Brunswick County, was one of the brave mothers of the Sixties, and though she was an invalid when her husband died and her two sons volunteered for the war, she courageously kept the "home fires burning." She lived to be ninety-one years old.

Early in the war a wayside hospital was established by the State Medical Department at Wilson, among other towns accessible to the railroad. The women of this little town, with their usual enthusiasm (which has endured until today), responded with aid societies at the first call for troops. The Wilson Light Infantry was one of the honorable military organizations in North Carolina before the war, and the girls of Wilson were busy equipping these boys.

At the end of the war when everything was in chaos the women were terrified because the town came very nearly being burned, owing to the fact that two Yankee prisoners had been put to death by Wheeler's men. The quick, cool command of the situation by Mr. George W. Blount, the mayor, saved these women and children their homes, as the Federals were made to see that the citizens of the town were not responsible.

Reign of Terror in Elizabeth City

*"They played their part 'mid saddening scenes,
War's cloud on land and sea."*

We have read of the sufferings of the women of New Bern, Washington, Fayetteville, and many other places of our beloved State, but the women of Elizabeth City in its reign of terror have few rivals in the agony of the Sixties. That gifted historian, Col. Richard Creecy, has left us a vivid picture of the trying period before and during the bombardment of Elizabeth City, early in February, 1862. The women of this town had zealously cared for the wounded and sick from Roanoke Island and Hatteras, and when the outrage to life and property began they felt paralyzed. As the bombardment began these delicately matured women bravely started for the country to seek places of safety. They were afoot, shoe tops deep in mud and slush, bedraggled, wretched. Mrs. Elliott and Mrs. Martin, with their children, started on foot for Oxford, while many mothers were vainly looking for their children amongst the terrible pandemonium. The worst features of human nature were developed on every side with its horrors of bummers, pillage, and rapine. This was a dark and bloody occasion and has scarcely a parallel in the State's history. How these women of the Albemarle section lived through those days will never be known. All honor to them.

The ladies of the beautiful home Cedar Vale took part in an important event that occurred in the vicinity of Elizabeth City. These ladies entertained one hundred Confederate prisoners after effecting their escape from a Federal transport which was carrying them to a Northern fortress.

Landing at Cape Henry, after they had seized the ship which was manned by twenty Federal officers, these hundred Confederates crossed the Pasquotank River, going on through the swamp, and landed on Yeopin Creek, back of Cedar Vale.

All the women in the neighborhood sent provisions of all kinds to these poor soldiers, besides sending cars and wagons to hasten them on their way. [The soldiers] were carried by river to the railroad, thence on to Richmond.

An interesting incident is given to us by Mrs. Molly E. Fearing of Elizabeth City:

"My husband, Capt. Fearing, had charge of Fort Barstow at Roanoke Island and made a brave resistance. He stood by his gun until blood ran from his ears and nose but he did not stop fighting. Gen. Burnside, the Federal commander, said, "Bring me that plucky little rebel, I want to see him and introduce him to my staff." There was a Fearing on Gen. Burnside's staff also. A few months later, as my husband was on a furlough from his wounds, he was arrested for a Confederate spy. Just as they were ready to put him to death a captain from Burnside's staff happened to come up and recognize Capt. Fearing, said, "I will answer for this man; he is not a spy, he is a regular commissioned officer in the Confederate service."

My mother had a most exciting time when she ran the blockade to get quinine and sugar for her children, leaving a six-week-old baby at home. She was stopped at the line of pickets, who said her pass was not for the whole way.

Though we have mentioned a number of the towns and communities who bore the brunt of warfare, yet there are many communities, especially along the coast, which suffered more than history can ever record. The women who heard the boom of cannons of Federal gunboats every night, as they sang their babies to sleep, little knew whether their home would be shelled before morning.

Around Edenton and the Albemarle Section

(The Ironclad Ship "Albemarle" Christened by Miss Spottswood)

Miss Mary E. Moore, one of our honored "Daughters" from Edenton, gives these interesting recollections of the northeastern part of the State.

"I have been requested to furnish some reminiscences from this section of the War between the States. Reluctantly, I draw aside the veil of the past and live over again those dark days of the Sixties that met me at the threshold of womanhood.

"For months our country had been in the throes of unrest; rumors of war from all sides that finally culminated in the bombardment of Fort Sumter, that ushered in the cruelest war of the nineteenth century. Father against son, brother against brother, friend against friend.

> "The time is long past—
> The scene is afar"

and many incidents of those times have faded from my memory, but there are others burnt into my brain that can never fade.

"I recall one bright April day in 1861, the militia of the company gathered on our green to raise companies to defend the homes our fathers gave us and claim the State's rights that are ours. Addresses were made explaining the issues of the day, while enrolling officers wrote the names of volunteers eager for the fray. Now and again they met with a snag, as I recall this incident an officer, book in hand, approached a youngster who had probably never before been out of sight of home, for those were not the days of automobiles, 'Come, my boy, give us your name and we will make a soldier of you.' 'No, sirree, I don't want to fight.' 'Why man, your honor is involved, what is life worth without your honor?' 'Wuth! what's my life wuth!, why it's wuth a heap.' With great disgust the poor officer turned away and said, 'Well, in Heaven's name, go home and enjoy it.'

"We raised two full companies, one for six months, commanded by Capt. James K. Marshall; the other commanded by Capt. T. L. Skinner, enlisted for the war, had the proud distinction of being mustered in as Company A, 1st Regiment

North Carolina State Troops. Of these many never returned. Their captain and first lieutenant fell near Richmond and lie buried in St. Paul's Church yard, Edenton. The strength of our manhood gone, the old men and boys, some only twelve and fourteen, formed a home guard, doing picket and courier duty, and running the blockade with what we could raise to help feed the army, for with the fall of Roanoke, we were in Yankee lines, our waters often filled with gunboats, and the only way we could reach what we called Dixie was by running the blockade across Chowan River.

"General Beauregard's call for the bells to be cast into cannon which gave rise to the beautiful poem, 'Melt the Bells,' met with prompt response, and quickly were gathered together the Episcopal and Methodist bells, town clock, Academy and shipyard dinner bells, preserving kettles, everything that contained bell metal and shipped [them] to Richmond, [to be] cast into cannon, formed into a battery and manned by our native boys, under the command of Capt. William Bedham. They did good service, never suffered defeat, [and were] surrendered at the close of the war. The last shot fired by old St. Paul['s] was picked up by one of the company, and now rests as a priceless treasure in the vault of St. Paul's Church, Edenton. The Baptist bell was not given, not from any want of patriotism, but it was built into the spire of the church, which required carpenters to take it down—we had none, they were all where they should have been, at the front.

"These were dark days, but we women worked on and hoped on, till our noble Stonewall Jackson fell, when we felt the die was cast.

"There were many incidents I might recall, for memory's storehouse holds many, some ludicrous, some pathetic—did I not fear I might grow prolix, for I have yet to tell the most important of all: the naval battle I witnessed on our beautiful Albemarle Sound.

"May the 5th, 1864, Capt. Cook, commander of the *Albemarle*, more familiarly known as the *Ram*, steamed down the Roanoke River, followed in the distance by two tenders, the *Bombshell* and the *Cotton Plant*. Soon the Yankee squadron, seven well-armed gunboats, the *Mattabessett*, the *Sassacus*, the *Wyhisine*, the *Whitehead*, the *Miami*, the *Com. Hull*, and the *Ceres*, hove in sight, Capt. Smith in command. At two o'clock, they approached in double line of battle, the *Mattabessett* in advance. They proceeded to surround the *Albemarle* and hurled at her their heaviest shot, only about one hundred yards away. The *Albemarle* responded at once, but her boats were soon shot away and [her] smokestack riddled. Still she fought on, though one of her guns was silenced and [its] steel plating broken. The *Sassacus* kept in constant motion, coming nearer each time, till, seizing her best opportunity, with all steam on, rammed the *Albemarle* just above the water mark, causing every timber to creak, and near sent her to the bottom with all on board. Soon our brave little gunboat righted herself and fired a broadside at her enemy, with such telling effect, tearing its way through from stem to stern, bursting her boiler, scalding to death seven of her men and wounding many others.

"Thus the battle kept up till five o'clock, when we saw the *Albemarle* slowly steaming back to the mouth of the river, not beaten for she still held her own, but her fuel was exhausted, and to keep up steam to reach Plymouth necessitated tearing away all inside woodwork which together with bedding, clothing, and provisions, was cast into the furnace. Thus our brave little *Albemarle* escaped capture and landed at Plymouth, covered with wounds and with glory.

"The war was nearing its close, though some of our bloodiest battles were yet to be fought. We were worn out, and in April, 1865, overcome by numbers, and to save further sacrifices of life, our ever faithful Lee, grand even in defeat, surrendered.

"Soon the remnants of our army reached home with

> "Broken hearts and broken hopes
> But now 'tis Auld Lang syne."

"Never again will the Stars and Bars wave over the Southern Confederacy. That dream is past. The Blue and the Gray are merged into the Khaki, worn by our boys overseas, where bearing aloft the Stars and Stripes, the proudest flag that floats over land and sea, they turned the tide of battle in the great world war."

Miss Lena H. Smith, the historian of the U.D.C. Chapter, Scotland Neck, has written a most interesting story of the building of the ironclad *Albemarle*. Her father, Peter E. Smith, had charge of the construction of this famous North Carolina vessel, and her uncle, Gilbert Elliott, the finances. Miss Smith tells of the launching of this vessel at its navy yard on the river below Halifax. This was an occasion of great importance, and Miss Mary Spottswood was the Sponsor who christened the ship by breaking a bottle of wine on her prow and naming her the *Albemarle*.

HEROIC WOMEN OF WESTERN NORTH CAROLINA

*"For they were loyal, and they were brave,
And we can now but speak their praise."*

The women of the western part of North Carolina were amongst the most heroic and loyal of our State, ever ready for noble work in the Confederacy.

While the women of the eastern and central part of North Carolina were suffering every indignity and persecution at the hands of Sherman's "bummers," the women further west were enduring similar treatment from Gen. Stoneman and Col. Kirk's troops. There are hundreds of cases in which real heroism was shown.

When the men of western North Carolina joined the forces of the Confederate army, their womenfolk were not only left unprotected within the line of battle or the famous March of Sherman to the Sea, but were in danger of those unprincipled men who could not join either side and laid out to evade the law and lived by robbing women on whom the responsibility of providing food and clothing for their children rested.

This thrilling story is given by Dr. Archibald Henderson, of the University of North Carolina, who received it from the lips of his grandmother, Mrs. William Cain (Sarah Jane Bailey), a daughter of Judge Lancaster Bailey, of Asheville, N.C.

"In March 1865, anticipating trouble for the town of Asheville, and its inhabitants, Gen. James G. Martin, advanced to meet the Federal commander, Gen. Gillam, in order to make the best terms possible. The meeting was cordial, and about noon the Northern detachment marched away. After supper that night, the Bailey family heard a terrible noise and discovered that it was Northern marauders from Gillam's division, who were riding up on the porch on horseback. They smashed open the glass doors of the verandah and struck heavily upon the head of the venerable Judge Bailey, who had seized a gun to drive them back. They rifled the trunks and boxes; took the wedding rings of mother and daughter, as well as wedding gifts, jewelry, and gold and silver coins which they found—all the while screaming, threatening, [and] yelling, with brandished torches. Thomas Bailey, the judge's son, surrendered to save his father's life and went along with the Yankee banditti as their prisoner. They wanted to return and "kill the old man," but were dissuaded by their prisoner. Nevertheless they returned and fired several shots through the door at the courageous old judge, who narrowly escaped his life. Next morning, several villainous-looking Yankees came and took away the family's supply of bacon. The judge was insulted on the street by a negro in blue uniform; Mrs. Henry Middleton literally fought with the Yankee soldiers in the effort to prevent them from stealing her husband's watch; and Mrs. James W. Patton, who was wearing her watch, was choked almost to death by a Yankee soldier who tore it from her.

"Thomas Bailey was not unkindly treated by his captors; and doubtless because of the inconvenience of guarding him, they released him before reaching Tennessee. There prevailed in Asheville a reign of terror, however. Negro troops under Gen. Howley committed nameless atrocities in the neighborhood of Asheville; and those apprehended were tried by drumhead court martial, and four of them shot. Judge Bailey went to see the Federal Gen. Brown, to protect against the outrageous conduct of his troops; but, although profuse in promises to remedy matters, the befuddled general was too intoxicated to remember to keep them. Eventually a young Federal officer, of a Michigan company, was secured as a personal guard; and under his kind and efficient guard, further outrages were prevented."

Mrs. James W. Patton and her sister, of Asheville, were dragged from their sick beds, their persons searched, and their valuables taken.

Some of the bravest, most cheerful women of the Confederacy were the wives of seven Irish men who entered the army from their settlement near Round Knob, where they had been employed on the unfinished railroad to the mountains. Every week two of these women walked eighteen miles over a rough road, to Asheville, to ask for help for the destitute families of that vicinity. Mrs. Nicholas Woodfin, one of Asheville's splendid workers, set aside a room for their use where they could rest after their arduous journey and assisted them in "collecting." These Irish women, by their amusing wit, gave moral support and cheer to many women who were of a higher social sphere.

One woman of Buncombe County, who was alone with five children and an old colored man, had finished her winter's supply of cloth and thread and was making a pot of dye in the yard one day so that the cloth could be dyed and dried before the night of the following day. After boiling her bark or leaves she had removed it from the liquid and was coming from the house with a handful of the precious copperas to thoroughly dissolve overnight, when she saw a group of men approaching.

These men were a band of the much-dreaded robbers. They forced the woman, children, and colored man to sit quietly while they tore all the blankets from the beds, [and] took her best clothes and all of the baby's clothes, her choicest dishes, and the undyed cloth and thread. Nothing was left her but the pot of liquid and the remains of the copperas, which had nearly all melted in her clenched hand.

Miss Emma L. Rankin, one of Lenoir's most beloved women, who has gone to rest, has left a host of interesting experiences of Stoneman's raid. This article has been preserved in a memorial booklet of this sainted woman of the Sixties. While occupying the position of honored teacher in Col. Logan Carson's house near Marion, McDowell County, Miss Rankin felt the full terror of Stoneman's raid through western North Carolina, when (with two defenseless women and children) they stood their ground courageously while the ruffians pointed pistols at their heads, making terrible threats of what they would do if they did not disclose the hiding place of hidden treasures. One of the gang set fire to the house to frighten the ladies, but extinguished it when they saw the bravery they exhibited. When night came on with all the terrors of darkness, these intrepid women locked themselves into their rooms. In the middle of the night rough voices demanded with kicks and oaths that the door be opened. On forcing it open one insolently demanded a breast pin which Miss Rankin wore, saying that if she did not give it up that they would take it from her. Refusing, Miss Rankin picked up a large iron shovel from the fireplace saying, "You dare not touch me." "Dare not," he said, "I fear not God or man." "I fear God," she said, "and you cannot harm me." To the utter astonishment and relief of this courageous woman the ruffian retreated, leaving her weak-kneed and trembling, but thankful to God for her deliverance. Even these ruthless men could not fail to admire the splendid spirit of Miss Emma Rankin, who was an example of the faith, courage, and self-reliance of a good woman in the midst of danger. Her name is a loving household word in many homes, whose children she has brought nearer to God by her teachings.

In her [*Last Ninety Days of the War in North-Carolina*], Mrs. Cornelia Spencer gives incidents of courage of the women of western North Carolina.

Mrs. W. W. Scott, whose home was near Lenoir, was alone at her residence at the time Stoneman's Federal troops were moving from Caldwell to Burke County. A Federal soldier, heavily armed, rode up to the house and demanded food. While he was enjoying his meal, Mrs. Scott seized his carbine and threatened to shoot if he made an outcry, made him a prisoner, and turned him over to the house guard. Mrs. Scott was the mother of Mrs. W. W. Scott, Jr., formerly editor of the Lenoir *Topic*. Such fearlessness was found in many of our Confederate women, who were made of fortitude beyond belief.

Mrs. Vaughn, of Lenoir, drew a pistol to resist the marauders but was overpowered.

Mrs. Harper, another Lenoir lady, was ill in bed, and a brutal soldier placed a shovel full of red-hot coals by her side to make her disclose her hidden valuables.

Mrs. Boone Clark, of Lenoir, was seized by the throat and almost killed (with her little girl), the ruffians repeatedly calling her a liar and other degrading names.

The women of Salisbury and Rowan County did much to relieve the suffering of the Confederate soldiers, there being three hospitals in Salisbury where they worked untiringly. Mrs.

Mary A. Wrenn and her daughter, Miss Betty, had charge of the largest of these hospitals, even selling their jewelry, silver, and other clothing to buy food for the patients.

Mrs. Montgomery had charge of the Wayside Hospital and Mrs. Jessie McCallum of the hospital at the old garrison. Besides [these,] there were many enthusiastic women workers among the sick and wounded.

The Soldiers' Relief Association of Rowan County was organized early in the war, with Mrs. D. A. Davis and Miss Camelia Brown as president and vice-president, and rendered valuable aid throughout the terrible four years.

Mrs. Sloan Johnston, a loyal Confederate, relieved the suffering not only of our Confederate soldiers but also the Federals imprisoned at Salisbury, and by her pleading secured the release of many prominent Salisbury men who were thrown into prison by Stoneman's raiders.

Gen. Stoneman destroyed not only the arsenal and foundry at Salisbury, but the public stores (collected from Richmond, Columbia, Charlotte, [and] Danville) the length of four squares in flames. The women and children, for months half starved and half clothed, saw quantities of provisions burning in their streets like so much rubbish. All the precious medicines, valued at $100,000 in gold, were destroyed, leaving women and children helpless in sickness.

Mrs. Margaret E. Ramsay showed the spirit of these other courageous women when a Confederate soldier, as he was being fired on by Federals, fell on her piazza. Though the balls fell thick about her, and [she was] alone with her little children, she went out to him and managed to get him inside her house, where she nursed and stimulated him through the day until the physician could arrive, and assisted in a surgical operation.

The home of Mrs. Frank Shobert was invaded and the brutal soldiers dashed into the privacy of her bed room, demanding her valuables. This gentle, loving woman lay in bed with her infant beside her, a few days old. After looting the house, as the soldiers departed one of them was shot by a Confederate on the piazza of Mrs. Shobert's home.

A mile out from Salisbury a train was fired on without any demand for surrender, and among the ladies on board were the widow and daughter of Gen. Leonidas Polk. The cars being set on fire, the ladies were forced to see their luggage burned, in which were cherished relics of Gen. Polk.

The women of High Point and Statesville, half starved too, saw quantities of provisions destroyed when the Yankees fired the Confederate government stores there. It was said the Iredell County women were almost all in mourning, as no county suffered more in the loss of her best and bravest sons in the Confederate army. The Yankees deprived the women along their western route of the comfort of their decrepit old men and very young boys by marching them off as prisoners. The women of Lenoir were vehemently cursed for giving food to these starved and exhausted old men, when they halted over night in this "rebellious little hole," as the Yankees called Lenoir.

In Statesville, it is recorded that the room of a woman in childbirth was even invaded, the brutality not stopping even on the threshold of life.

The fearless Mrs. James Camcill, of Wataugua County, after repeated insults was made a prisoner in her own home, by Kirk.

Mrs. Paxton, near Morganton, was locked in her room and tortured for not disclosing her valuables.

WIT AND REPARTEE

"Woman's wit is greater than man's wisdom."

"Wit is precious as the vehicle of sense."

Many clever sayings have been handed down from these women of the Sixties, full of humor and wit, that show their spirit and brilliancy. We know of a young "tar heel" girl, a brilliant talker, [who] while her home was being pillaged by Sherman's "bummers" made a speech narrating the cause of the war, its beginning in the days of nullification and secession, quoting John C. Calhoun's speech in Congress down on through until Sherman's men reached her own home. The soldiers closed about her listening, their hands unconsciously dropping the articles they had stolen. As she ceased they said to her, "We never knew the South had so much to fight for, if we had we would never draw gun or sword."

The courage displayed even by the young girls in the Confederacy was wonderful, and often their bright answers, even in the face of personal danger, showed a spirit that couldn't be put down, showing that woman's wit is greater than man's wisdom. While the Yankees were burning the home of Rev. Colin Shaw, in Bladen County (he being away at the front and the only inmates being three defenseless women), Miss Mollie Shaw, his lovely eighteen-year-old daughter, sat at her piano playing her beloved "Dixie," until the flames almost enveloped her.

When Federal officers had their headquarters in the grove of Sharon, the home of Dr. Jonathan North (then state treasurer), they asked his charming young daughter, Miss Mary, to play while they sang the Northern song, "Tramp, Tramp, Tramp, the Boys are Marching," whereupon she replied that she would do so, but she would transpose the verses into those with Southern words.

On another occasion when the Yankees were occupying the refugee country home of Miss Nellie Worth, of Wilmington, she was compelled by them to play the piano. She vowed to herself she would play nothing but Southern songs, so surrounded by her "deadly enemies" (to quote her) "I cooly sang 'The Bonnie Blue Flag' and 'Dixie' with all my might, breathing intense fire and hate in my soul in those two songs."

Mrs. Croaker was a Kinston character noted for her repartee. A Yankee chaplain told her that God had sent freedom as a gift to the slaves.

"That might be so," she replied, "but if it is, the devil came to bring the gift."

He quoted Sherman's famous "War is Hell." She said, "Sherman ought to know his native customs. I suppose he knows all there is to know about hell. It's his home talk."

Mrs. Polly Chadwick of New Bern one day saw a Federal soldier drummed out of his regiment with a board strapped on his back and the word "thief" on it. She called out, "What has the poor fellow done?" "Been stealing." "Stealing," said Mrs. Polly, "why, if you drummed out all who stole, there would not be pine trees enough in North Carolina to furnish planks for their backs."

An old lady of Fayetteville was seated at a dinner party with the Federal officers who were occupying her home. "General," she said, to quote her own words, "'Ain't you going to ask a blessing?' 'Well, Grandma,' he replied, 'I don't know how, won't you do it for me?' So I asked a blessing and prayed a short prayer. I asked the Lord to turn their hearts away from their wickedness and make them go back to their homes and stop fighting us, and everything I was afraid to tell them I told the Lord and they couldn't say a word."

Miss Sarah Ann Tillinghast, of Fayetteville, showed her Puritan ancestry when she stood on her doorsteps, while her house was being ransacked, and with true Puritan fervor read for the benefit of her unwelcome Yankee visitors the 108th Psalm, wherein the Psalmist commends the thought that the days of the unmerciful "be few" and that their names be "blotted out."

These stories are told by the "old inhabitants" of Fayetteville:

Gen. Sherman came to Fayetteville by the Camden road, and on his way stopped at the old Nelson house on that road, in the Rockfish section of what was then Cumberland County, now Hoke County. Here took place a very pretty little dialogue between the famous commander and Mrs. Nelson, the proud and defiant mistress of the house. The day was March 10th; and in greeting the invader Mrs. Nelson informed that the 10th of March was a momentous day in her life.

First was the visit of General LaFayette in 1824, when he stopped at her house and kissed her hand. On that day in 1845 three persons lay dead in her house, one being a brother slain by his brother's hand. "And now, on March 10th, 1865," she added, "you come with your robbers, to rob us." "Madam," replied Gen. Sherman, "I assure you that we will not rob you or harm you in any way, and, further, I, too, shall kiss your hand." And he did. And Mrs. Nelson was not robbed.

Another maiden lady of Cumberland County, Miss Margaret Shaw, one of the "salt of the earth," showed her spirit when after occupying her home for the night, the Yankee officer asked if he could bury his men in her field. She replied, "with the greatest pleasure." On being asked by her invited guests, the Yankee soldiers, on how she felt that morning, she replied, "I feel like David did when the hosts of hell were encamped round about him."

Not far from Fayetteville there lived an elderly maiden lady, who when she heard that Sherman's "bummers" were coming, hid her jewelry and silver. When the bummers arrived they commanded her to tell them where she had hidden her treasures. When she refused they caught her and choked her until they thought she would yield. When she was released and had caught her breath, she asked, "Why, do you think, did I hide my things from you?"

"To keep us from getting them, of course," was the reply.

"Then, don't you think I'd be a fool to tell you where I hid them? I'll never tell you if you choke me to death."

They left her, but the purple marks of their clutches were on her throat for several days afterwards.

In the McNeill family there were several daughters ranging from sixteen to twenty-four years of age. When Sherman's army arrived a neighbor came to Mr. McNeill and asked him to bring the young ladies to his home, as several officers were quartered there and that he had procured a guard from them and they would be comparatively safe. The invitation was gladly accepted. One afternoon while officers, young ladies of the family, and visitors were all sitting together on the piazza, a negro near who belonged to Mr. McNeill came to the steps and asked one of the ladies to show him the officer who had charge of the grist mill on the premises. Then very humbly, with hat in hand, the negro said to the officer, "Your soldiers have taken everything we had to eat, and my mistress sent me to ask you for some corn meal to make bread for the children." The officer in a very lordly way announced, "Well, suppose I don't give it to you, what would you do?"

"We'll have to trust in Providence, sir," said the negro.

"Didn't you know that Providence died some time ago?" said the officer.

"Yes-sah, I knows he did, but he riz agin," was the humble answer.

There was some clapping from the "rebel" part of the audience but the negro got his meal.

LITERARY WOMEN OF THE SIXTIES

"Sound judgment the ground of writing well."

*"A perfect Woman, nobly planned,
To warn, to comfort, and command."*

It has been said of Mrs. Cornelia Phillips Spencer that she was like some jewel, "full of fire."

The work of this brilliant woman stands out differently from that of any other of North Carolina's women of the Sixties.

Her *Last Ninety Days of the War [in North-Carolina]*, written in '66 (at the request of Governor Vance), is invaluable as a vivid and true picture of those last terrible days and the beginning of the Reconstruction period in this State. This history, a classic, depicts North Carolina's part in the struggle and is one of the greatest things accomplished by any of our women of that day, being written by one who saw and endured an active part in this great drama. Her children's history of North Carolina is also a true story of the State.

Mrs. Hope Summerell Chamberlain, in her recent book *Old Days in Chapel Hill*, has made a valuable contribution to the literary history of this period of our State, by compiling the journals and letters of Mrs. Spencer. She has recalled to the present generation the splendid services of this woman of the Sixties, "who was the equal in intellect and worth of any other woman in America." Mrs. Chamberlain says that the idea in writing this book was to show Northern readers that Sherman's campaign methods and those of others were unnecessarily severe and harsh, and to give as much well authenticated personal experience as possible from all over the State. Mrs. Spencer has left to the State many letters and newspaper articles which are of great literary and historical value.

Her services to her State during these dark days were direct and personal, having been friend and counselor of Governor Vance (redeemer of the State from Reconstruction) and other of the State's readers, who sought her advice frequently. [As she was] a resident of Chapel Hill, many of the brilliant men who attended the University during and following the war were influenced by her remarkable personality, and through them she contributed greatly toward shaping the destinies of North Carolina. Her great work was denouncing the outrages of Reconstruction and calling aloud, with her pen, to the people to be steadfast, brave, and true. To her was due, largely, the overthrow of the carpetbagger and his exodus from the State.

She wrote and spoke and prayed unceasingly for the overthrow of the foul gang that were polluting her beloved University hall in these Reconstruction days. The University, which had remained open through all the horrors of the war, was closed to students and the dormitories were turned into stables for horses of cutthroat Federal soldiers sent to overcome the Southern people in their resistance to carpetbag government. Cornelia Spencer thundered, through the press of the State, defiance to oppressive authority, and to the sons of the University everywhere she uttered rallying cries for the revival of this seat of learning.

Her labors and prayers were answered, and she saw the

University restored to its own, a day of triumph for her to whom was most due (except Dr. Kemp Battle) its reopening.

Throughout the four dreary years of the war she encouraged and cheered the students who remained at Chapel Hill, being their comrade and counselor, besides working for the soldiers who were away fighting and caring for many needy families.

The downfall of her State brought forward Mrs. Spencer's remarkable ability; [her] knowledge of men and events in North Carolina in its critical period of war and Reconstruction was greater than that of any man or woman of that day. Her name should be placed high in the history of North Carolina's women of the Sixties.

In her book, *The Last Ninety Days of the War in North-Carolina*, Mrs. Spencer pays this tribute to her fellow women of the Confederacy.

"When I forget you, O ye daughters of my country, your labors of love, your charity, faith, and patience, all through the dark and bloody day; lighting up the gloom of war with tender graces of women's devotion and self-denial, and now in your energy and cheerful submission in toil and poverty and humiliation; when I cease to do homage to your virtues and your excellencies, may my right hand forget its coming, and my voice be in silent dust."

"Sing me the songs that to you were so dear, long, long ago."

Mrs. Frances Fisher Tiernan, of Salisbury, known to the literary world as "Christian Reid," has given a name to add to the State's women of the Sixties of which we are justly proud.

Her father was Col. Charles F. Fisher, who as commander of the 6th North Carolina Regiment gave his life at the first battle of Manassas. Out of her sorrow in his death (though in her teens) grew her love for the Confederacy, and the history of the South was a passion with her. She was the first historian of the North Carolina Division, U.D.C., and until her death, honorary president. She gave of her unquenchable spirit to keep history straight in the Southern cause, and placed the gifts of her mind, heart, and pen at the service of the South, writing that beautiful and stirring war drama, *Under the Southern Cross*.

This was later played before scores of Southern audiences, resulting in the creation of many enduring monuments in bronze and stone to the memory of that perfect army of our Confederacy.

As a novelist we halo her name in especial administration for the true and perfect pictures she drew of our Confederacy, and we Daughters of today owe a deep debt to her for her contribution to the Southern Cause.

The soldiers of her father's regiment adored her, and at the sight of her and the mention of her name they would almost stampede the house.

In 1874 with one stroke of her pen, "Christian Reid" gave North Carolina the name by which it was to become famous around the world—*The Land of the Sky*—by a most delightful book describing most vividly the grandeur of our mountains. The greatest literary honor ever paid "Christian Reid" was the presentation to her of a gold medal by a distinguished French Literary Society after her story, "The Lady Dela Crucis," had been translated into French. She was also made a member of the exclusive society The Order of the Golden Rose of France. It has been said of her that "she was like unto a harp of a thousand strings vibrating with harmony, music falling from every string, the cadence lingering to charm the ear, dying never but living on and on down the ages."

There is nothing more powerfully dramatic and compelling than her wonderful patriotic poem "Gloria Victis," a hymn of triumphant victory in honor of the Confederate soldiers' bravery. Her poem "Regret," a refrain of the heart, is considered by many one of the finest poems by any North Carolinian. Her [novel] *Valerie Aylmer*, written in the Sixties, [a] refrain of the heart, considered by many one of the finest poems by [her] while she was still a young woman, stands today a work of art in the literary world.

When the world war came no one was more devoted to the Allied cause than she. Though ill and scarcely able to leave her room, she made some of the most inspiring speeches given in Salisbury, being a gifted public speaker.

Mrs. Mary Bayard Clarke, a daughter of Thomas Polk Devereux, of Raleigh, was a literary genius of the Sixties, of whom North Carolina is very proud. This typical Confederate woman, whom both Raleigh and New Bern claimed, used her pen with poetry and prose in telling the story of the South, her work as a poet being especially valuable. [As t]he wife of a Confederate soldier, Col. William J. Clarke, her heart was with the South and the Old North State always, and in verse she poured forth the sufferings and glory of the Confederacy. It has been said that one of her poems, "Must I Forget," is not excelled by Byron, and that she was akin to Wordsworth in style. Her poem "General Lee at the Battle of the Wilderness" has a note of the sublime, while "Rebel Sock" contains a humorous touch. Her *Social Reminiscences of Noted North Carolinians* is a collection of interest, and her *[Wood-notes:] Carolina Carols* ([compiled] in 1854) contain fine contributions of her own as well as of others. Mrs. Clarke also contributed to *The Land We Love* one of the most interesting of her writings being her character sketch from the life of "Aunt Abby, the Irrepressible."

Mrs. Clarke's pen name in poetry was "Tenella," and in prose "Stuart Leigh."

During the Reconstruction period she supported many who were in need, by her writings.

Miss Sarah Ann Tillinghast, of Fayetteville, in '65 gave to the South a beautiful poem "Answer to the Conquered Banner," a fit mate to Father Ryan's famous poem telling us to "Love it, [keep] it for its past."

Her poem "Carolina's Dead" was written as a Memorial Day ode to our fallen heroes, and is a beautiful tribute to the men in gray.

Miss Tillinghast wrote many interesting sketches of war days in her community and was noted for her witty answers to the Yankees when they were occupying Fayetteville.

Mrs. Fannie Downing has left some beautiful verses which were published in *The Land We Love*, a magazine edited by Gen. D. H. Hill, just after the war. Her "Memorial Flowers" is a lengthy and charming poem that breathes the love every Southern woman feels for Memorial Day. Her "Reconstruction" is also a poem of real literary merit, as [are] numbers of others that have been loved and admired. Mrs. Downing, though a native of Virginia, came to this State as a young woman, to make her home in Mecklenburg County.

Mrs. A. L. [i.e., V. L. (Victoria Louise)] Pendelton, of Warrenton, has contributed greatly to the literary and historical work of this State, since a girl in the Sixties. This lady of eighty-nine is a living page from the Old South, and her literary style is beautiful and fine. Besides many poems of real merit, her booklet entitled *Last Words of Confederate Heroes* is filled with tributes to these men who fought with Lee.

The daughter of Mrs. Pendelton, Mrs. Kathrine Arrington, is to place the name of this devoted real "Daughter of the Confederacy" on a bronze tablet in the Memorial Hall at Stone Mountain [Ga.,] a most deserved tribute to the one who has for years given of her best to her Southland, and since its organization an ardent [member of the] U.D.C.

As a young woman in the Confederacy, Mrs. Pendelton endured hardships and self-sacrifices, and her recollections of the Sixties are told in a most interesting way. In describing a journey from Greenville to Warrenton, during the war, Mrs. Pendelton says she and her sister had to sit on boxes in a freight car surrounded by sides of bacon. Her brother remarked, as he lifted her in the car, "You have been contemplating a trip to Europe, and you ought to be happy now for you are in the middle of Greece."

Mrs. Pendelton gives these lines as a preface to her *Last Words of Confederate Heroes:*

> "The men who went to the tented field,
> And the women who bade them never to yield
> To the invading foe, are passing away—
> Ah! few of our heroes are living today;

Few women who waited, and wept and wrought
Are left now to tell how bravely they fought.
We exulted o'er victories, wept at defeat,
And 'lest we forget,' I here will repeat
The last words of heroes on whom we relied,
For nobly they lived and nobly they died."

The first woman to edit a newspaper in North Carolina was Rachael Holton, who became the editor of the *North Carolina Whig*, formerly the *Charlotte Journal*, on the death of her husband, E. J. Holton, soon after the war began. This plucky woman felt that the paper should be continued at this critical period when news traveled so slowly, so she put her shoulder to the wheel and capably carried it on 'til '63, when it was discontinued on account of the scarcity of paper.

It is said that another reason for its ceasing publication was the fact that the chimney to the office fell down and there were no men available to put it back.

Nor did the women forget that their children should be educated though their fathers and brothers were at the front. Teachers were scarce, but many of our women filled the places vacated by the soldiers.

The boarding schools of St. Mary's, Raleigh, Greensboro, and Salem were kept open, as was the Charlotte Female Institute.

From the second volume of [Samuel] Ashe's valuable history of North Carolina we learn that as the supply of schoolbooks diminished, the efficient Mrs. Moore, of Raleigh, a daughter of the publisher, Mr. Branson, prepared a series of primers, readers, and other books for use in the schools. Printing paper was so scare that it is said that some books were printed on wallpaper.

Capt. Ashe gives this extract from the report of 1863 of the State Superintendent of Common Schools, Rev. Calvin H. Wiley. This should be remembered by our citizens of today.

"The future historian will add, as our crowning glory, that in the darkest hour of the Confederacy, when every nerve and muscle of the country were wrought to the highest tension in a terrible and unparalleled struggle for existence and independence, North Carolina still supported a vigorous and beneficient system of free and public schools, and that they were attended by 50,000 of the children of her patriotic citizens."

CHRISTMAS DURING THE CONFEDERACY

*"It's getting close to Chris'mus,
Wid the chillun feelin' spry."*

The ingenuity shown by our women in playing the part of Santa Claus shows that though their hearts were breaking over their men at the front, still they gave happiness to their children by devising many attractive gifts, "making something out of nothing."

In our call for reminiscences of "Christmas in the Confederacy," the delightful little glimpses of those days that have come from many of our survivors of that period, throughout the State, deserve a separate chapter in our "Women of the Sixties." In her story of Christmas in the Confederacy, Mrs. F. C. Roberts of New Bern has left us this charming peep into her home in the Christmas of '64:

"Dark clouds were gathered around us, but the star of hope shone bright above us, and our faith was steadfast and unwavering. The year had been a hard one. Our resources were at the lowest ebb when Christmas confronted us. Stockings must be filled, gifts must be ready, children's faith in Santa Claus must be sustained, and how could all this be accomplished? My husband was home from the army on sick leave. It taxed our ingenuity, but the little ones must not be disappointed. He was skilled in the use of tools and made a cradle for one, a carriage for another, and a cart for the little boy, while I ransacked trunks for odds and ends to make and dress dolls. They were, of course, rag dolls with cheeks painted with poke-berries, eyes with indigo, and hair with sumac berries.

"Our ground-pea patch had yielded well, and we had laid by late apples from our orchard; we had sorghum for candy and cakes. I had bartered a little salt for a dozen eggs. I drew people and animals on paper, and Mammy Caroline laid them on her dough and with a sharp knife cut them out, thus making a fine menagerie.

"On Christmas Eve the children, white and black, brought evergreens and berries from the woods to decorate the parlor, making it a bower of fragrance and beauty. I had been so fortunate as to obtain tallow enough to fill a set of tallow moulds. So, for my Christmas illumination I had twelve elegant 'dips,' an improvement on a lightwood torch. I found twelve empty bottles to serve as candlesticks. These I hid among the evergreens. The stockings were hung "by the chimney with care," and Santa came! Verily and truly he had come, for the children had covered the hearth with sand, and there on the sand were traces of his sleigh and the prints of the reindeers' feet.

"It requires very little to make children happy. On Christmas morning the house rang with their cries of 'Merry Christmas!' They were wild with delight. No expensive toys could have given more pleasure than the simple ones we had prepared for them. A big basket was filled with animal cakes, apples, and ground peas, and their nurses took them to the Quarters to distribute the contents to the little negroes. The older servants had the same, with the addition of cider for the women and something stronger for the men. It was the best we could do and they seemed content.

"Our dinner was frugal. It consisted of rice and peas in many forms with a desert of delicious cake, wine, ground peas, and apples. My cake was made of dried cherries, dried whortle berries, candied watermelon rind, and sorghum. When we returned to the parlor the candles had been lighted. Here our guests took leave of us, and here ended one Christmas day in the Confederacy."

Another recollection of Christmas in the Sixties is from Mrs. A. McA. Gainey of Cumberland County, who recalls her childhood days.

"My Christmas of 1863 was a very happy one. Old Santa Claus gave me simple gifts but just as jolly as those in which my grandchildren of today are receiving.

"On this special Christmas morning what should I find in 'my box'? A complete little loom Santa Claus had made with his own knife, a cornstalk bed with a rag doll in it which Mrs. Santa Claus had made, were right there. My brother found to his delight a little wagon with spool wheels and a small wooden box body. His flute, which furnished the noise for the day, was made from a river lowland reed. But its tones were much more agreeable than the racket boxes we now have.

"Were our stockings bulged from toe to top with apples, oranges, raisins, nuts, and store-bought candy? Oh! No! Mrs. Santa Claus had been a very diligent, industrious, resourceful lady and had made ample provision for the satisfying of our 'sweet tooth.' She had in each of our boxes a nice package of molasses and honey candy which was full of big, nice, black walnut goodies, and ginger cookies cut by her deft hands to strikingly resemble animals we knew.

"Oh, yes! our Christmas was much more simple and our toys handmade; but let no one for one minute think we were not pleased with them and far happier than the present-day child who is ever wanting more."

The story of our "Women of the Sixties" would not be complete without mentioning the old colored "mammies." What would our Confederate women have done without the fidelity of these dear old loyal souls? Wherever her duties, in the field, kitchen, at the tub, spinning the wheel, nursing "de children" or waiting on "de big house," mammy did her part faithfully and lovingly, often being the comforter to her mistress when sad news came and sorrowing with the family in their grief.

Miss Georgia Hicks has written a beautiful reminiscence of her old colored "mammy," Cynthia Hill. When all the other negroes of Col. Hill, of Faison, had gone or been driven away, Cynthia came to the house and told her old "Marster" she wanted to stay with him. Col. Hill told her that she could and that he would care for her. She remained with the Hill family for over sixty years, and her pride was great in her "white folks," to whom she was devoted. She was loved by all the children of the village, and their greatest joy was to hear Cynthia tell tales of "before de war." During the last days of Mrs. Hill's life Cynthia was her faithful bodyguard, and when at last her spirit passed to the Beyond, this faithful old "slave" was buried in the family plot of the Hills, and her pallbearers were the boys (now grown to manhood) whom she had nursed in their infancy.

Women Urge Church Bells for Confederate Cannon

The women of the Confederacy felt that their cause was righteous, holy, and sacred and involved the highest duty and dearest sacrifice of devoted Christians. So when they urged that their precious church bells should be given to the Confederate government for making cannon for our army, this was the most significant illustration of their devotion to the Southland.

A valuable and beautiful bit of history in which the Confederate women of the State had their part is that which has been collected by Mrs. Henry Armand London, of Pittsboro (an ex-president of the North Carolina Division, U.D.C.). As chairman of the U.D.C. committee on "Church Bells in the Confederacy," Mrs. London gave this report at the annual State convention in 1920.

"In view of the scarcity of tin and other metal suited to the manufacture of field artillery in the Confederacy, and in compliance with the call of the Ordnance Review in Richmond for bells early in 1862, many churches patriotically gave their bells to the Confederate government to be cast into cannon.

"In Hillsboro the Baptist, Presbyterian, and Saint Matthew['s] Episcopal churches gave their bells; the bell of this Episcopal church was used to make the cannon for the battery of the Hillsboro soldiers. After the war this was replaced by a memorial bell, given by Mrs. M. A. Curtis, in memory of her son John Henry Curtis, and his comrades from this town. All the churches in Washington gave their bells. The Roman Catholic and Presbyterian churches were burned by Yankees, while the Episcopal church was desecrated and used by the Yankees for barracks.

"The bell of St. John's Episcopal Church in Fayetteville was offered to the government by the vestry, April 1862, but was not accepted. The bell of the Presbyterian church of Fayetteville was offered by the session of the church in April 1862, but was not accepted on account of the difficulty of transportation.

"Edenton has the honor of four cannons that were cast from the bells in that town, and they became the Edenton Bell Battery, in the Confederacy. St. Paul's Episcopal Church bell, the Methodist Church bell, and the Academy bell were all given and cast into four cannons, namely, the 'St. Paul,' the 'Fanny Roulhac,' the 'Columbia,' and the 'Edenton.' These four cannons formed the battery that protected the sound from Yankee gunboats.

"The churches of Halifax all gave their bells. Mr. Thomas Pollock of that town had given a bell for the servants' chapel and they too offered their bell, which was sent with the others.

"The bells from St. Bartholomew's Church of Pittsboro, and Calvary Church of Tarboro, were also given.

"Weldon in '61 had only a little Union church, with no bell of its own, as it used the railroad shed bell for the call to service but the little chapel was used all through the war as a hospital for our soldiers.

"The Methodist and Episcopal churches of Plymouth also offered their bells, also the Methodist church at Greensboro.

"In Wilmington the St. James Episcopal Church was closed for divine worship by the Yankees, the pews and pulpit torn out with pickaxes, upon the refusal of its rector to pray for the president of the United States instead of the president of the Confederate States.

"In Charlotte all five churches gave their bells, which were melted into cannon for Brem's Battery, a Charlotte artillery organization. Almost the entire battery was lost at the battle of New Bern. Many guns, gun-carriages, and fittings were made at the Charlotte navy yard.

"After the war, when the Presbyterian church bell of Charlotte was replaced by a larger bell, inscribed on this was the history of this first bell.

"The five churches of Raleigh tendered their bells. On April 4, 1862, the Baptist church offered its large bell, which weighed thirteen hundred pounds and made three six-pounders, a half a battery.

"We copy from the *Raleigh Register* of April '62, these verses from a poem entitled 'The Church Bells of the Confederacy.'

> *Loosen the bolts—lower me down;*
>   *Cannon must be made.*
> *From hill and vale, and leaguered town*
>   *A Nation's call for aid!*
> *The joy of a country's heart is gone,*
>   *The light of a people fled;*
> *To hearts and hearths, the foe presses on*
>   *O'er the forms of the gallant dead.*
>
> *No more should the tongues of the village bell*
>   *Give forth its cheerful strain*
> *Till freedom and peace together shall dwell*
>   *In this fair sunny land again.*
> *So haste to the foundry, let me go,*
>   *Where my brazen sides may yield*
> *A weapon of death to the insolent foe*
>   *And then—away to the field!*
>
> *Transferred again to my lonely perch,*
>   *When the battle's fought and done—*
> *A peal I'll ring from the village church*
>   *For countless glories won.*
> *And anon—a song for the brave who bled,*
>   *Ere victory crowned the day.*
> *And a dirge for the names of the honored Dead,*
>   *Who fell in the fearful fray.*

OTHER CHARACTERS OF NORTH CAROLINA

The "First Lady" of North Carolina in the War

The "First Lady" in North Carolina during the greater part of the Confederacy was Mrs. Zebulon Vance, wife of our beloved War Governor. This frail little woman helped to equip companies and went through these terrible days by the side of her courageous husband, helping to inspire him with strength to guide wisely his "Ship of State." In unwavering faith, high spirit, strength, courage, and steadfastness of principle, she was an example to all other women of the State who were suffering and enduring.

With her four little sons, she was forced to flee from Raleigh, on the approach of Sherman's army, and all her trunks were broken open by these "bummers." Again when [she was] ill in bed in Statesville, her furniture and all belongings were taken by the Yankees, her children being left without even a bed, and again when [she was] ill, her husband was taken from her very arms to be imprisoned in Washington City. On all these terrible occasions this intrepid little woman showed an indominitable spirit, for which she was honored throughout North Carolina.

Though most modest and retiring in her nature, yet Mrs. Anna Morrison Jackson, of Charlotte, stands out amongst our fearless women, not only for herself but as the wife of our immortal Stonewall Jackson. She gave to the Confederacy her distinguished husband, whom she followed in many a battle, almost being in the fighting herself. On one occasion, when en route to the winter camp to join Gen. Jackson, she had packed full of provision for the soldiers a worn-out hair trunk. Some of our soldiers on the train were ridiculing the ancient article, whereupon the black mammy, who accompanied her, as nurse to little Julia, exclaimed, "Yo' better not be makin fun o' that ere trunk, 'cause hit belongs to Mrs. Stonewall Jackson." The Confederates at once apologized, with bows to the trunk.

Mrs. Jackson showed the spirit of her noble husband by helping to keep green the memory of the Confederacy in her memorial work and later in the U.D.C., being the honorary president of this Division.

Executive ability was displayed by so many of our women in those critical days. This characteristic was shown to a marked degree by Mrs. Jonathan Worth, of Asheboro, who was one of the "Inventive Women of the War." Her husband had equipped an entire company from his county, at his own expense, and Mrs. Worth herself oversaw all the garments made for these men.

Throughout the war she paid numbers of needy women in that vicinity to sew and knit for this company, this not only providing them with a livelihood but giving them happiness of working for their own husbands and fathers. Whenever soldiers would pass through the town, Mrs. Worth would have her servants go out and gather up the discarded socks left by the soldiers. After having them washed in steaming tubs, she would employ soldiers' wives to knit new feet on these clean socks, shipping them to the soldiers at the front. In '62, when Mr. Worth became State treasurer, under Gov. Vance, Mrs. Worth shared the responsibility of caring for the State's books, and later, when [he was] governor of North Carolina, she courageously went through the terrors of Reconstruction days by his side. By her dignified [tact] and good sense, she saved the day in many instances when the Yankee hordes were terrorizing Raleigh.

The memory of Mrs. Margaret Ann Cromwell, a sainted woman of the Sixties, hangs like a benediction to those who remember her wonderful personality and activities during the war. Margaret Ann Cromwell showed her heroic ancestry when she sent her young husband, Elisha Cromwell, to fight for the Confederacy, with a cheerful smile, then with an aching heart she went to work to do her part for the South and her soldiers. She was a helpmeet in truth, assisting Col. Cromwell in organizing his regiment.

Besides managing her large plantation, Margaret Cromwell was the "mother" of the company of boys that her husband carried to the war, spinning and weaving clothes, knitting, and in every way administering to their comfort.

Mrs. Cromwell was known throughout her native county, and adjoining counties, as a woman of strong, irreproachable character, and although raised in affluence, when the dark days of the war came, she ministered to those that were less fortunate than herself and was a friend indeed to the needy families of her soldiers. Mrs. Cromwell's self-forgetfulness gave inspiration to others, and to all she came in contact with she was a constant blessing. Her granddaughter, Mrs. Jackson Daniel Thrash Morrison, was one of the beloved ex-presidents of the North Carolina Division, U.D.C.

Like Mrs. Cromwell in incessant work for the Confederacy was Mrs. Tempie Ann (Battle) Marriott, of the same vicinity. Her husband, Dr. Marriott, not being physically able to serve in the army, did more than his share as physician and chief adviser to the people of Nash and Edgecombe counties. Mrs. Marriott did everything possible to aid the Cause by raising great quantities of provisions, which were given to feed her county's soldiers. She kept many of them clothed by her own work of spinning, weaving, and sewing. One of her four soldier brothers died of fever, but though heartbroken, this woman of the Sixties worked all the harder for her beloved South.

Her spirit of endeavor has been handed down to her granddaughter and namesake, Tempie Whitehead Holt, another past president of the North Carolina Division, U.D.C.

Mrs. Robert Ransom, the wife of one of North Carolina's distinguished generals, was a wealthy woman who came south with her husband from Washington City. She gave of her own means to help Gen. Ransom equip the 1st North Carolina [Cavalry], which he raised and trained at Ridgeway.

All during the war Mrs. Ransom sent boxes and did work for the sick soldiers. When married, she had dozens of suits of linen underwear and many linen shirts, etc. Many of these she scrapped to make lint for the hospitals. She lived with a most hospitable family five miles from Petersburg, and a large four-room office was always filled with sick soldiers whom she and the mistress of the home nursed. She would go to the other hospitals and write letters home for the men, and alas, too often writing to tell of their death. In the possession of her daughter, Mrs. F. M. Williams, is a letter from President Davis, thanking her for a box of provisions sent him, and saying they were almost on the verge of starvation when it came. She shipped boxes of honey from Maj. John Browning's farm, where she refugeed in '64. [After] the close of the war, in October '66, she opened a large school in Wilmington, and while she had charge of this she wrote President Davis, who had then lost everything, asking him to send her his oldest daughter, Maggie, and allow her to educate her. The letter making the offer has lately been published in the Collection of Letters and Papers of President Davis, arranged by Dr. Dembar Rowland, of Mississippi.

To her death Mrs. Ransom loved the South, and her agony at her husband's absence in the war was increased by the knowledge that her only brother and her only sister's husband were on the other side, and she dreaded them ever meeting.

Here is a recollection of Mrs. Fannie Ransom Williams, of her childhood while refugeeing:

"We had stopped somewhere for the night, and had no bread. Mother tried to buy some meal, but the negroes, and they were the only people in the number, would not sell us any, so our old mammy went out and got a little, I don't know how. Having nothing to mix with it, I remember going with 'Mammy' to pick up persimmons, which they baked in the corn meal we ate."

Truly the name of Mrs. Robert Ransom should be remembered as one of our "Women of the Sixties," as she gave her heart and means to the Southern Cause, though born beyond the Mason and Dixon Line. Her splendid spirit is inherited by her daughter, one of our honored ex-Division presidents, Mrs. Fannie Ransom Williams.

Mrs. William Parsley, Founder of the North Carolina Division, U.D.C.

TO MOTHERS OF THE U.D.C.
(By Mrs. Thomas M. Brockman)

With gallant stars a-glimmer
On a field of royal blue
As a guide and an inspiration,
Southern women, loyal and true,
Formed a circle wide as the heavens
Made a vow as firm as the stars,
To build a shrine forever
Round their hallowed Stars and Bars.

Then here's to the loyal women,
Of the State we love the best,
Who have kept alive through trying years
A page that will stand the test
Of all history's searchlights,
Of all that the years set free—
The women who sealed the heart of the South
In the shrine of the U.D.C.

One of the most beloved and honored of the North Carolina women of the sixties was Mrs. William M. Parsley (Eliza Hall Nutt), of Wilmington, "mother" and organizer of the North Carolina Division, U.D.C. Mrs. Parsley was made a widow of the Confederacy on April 6th, 1865, her gallant young colonel husband being killed three days before the surrender. State's rights, patriotism, and duty were her watchwords, and she continued after his death to live up to these principles. She realized it was her duty to help the worn-out and disabled soldiers, to encourage those who came from the war disheartened, to give them comfort and help them begin life anew. Knowing there were many worse off than herself she asked her father to help them, and accepted a position in a school. There she began the education of her two little girls.

In December, 1894, she organized the Cape Fear Chapter of the Daughters of the Confederacy, and in April, 1895, she organized the North Carolina Division of the United Daughters of the Confederacy, being unanimously elected its first president. Chapters and individuals went to her for guidance, and she urged all to teach the coming generation correct history: that the Southern soldiers were heroes and not traitors. She was literally a "mother" of the Confederacy, for she had loved, and suffered and lost. Her life was a benediction to many a soldier, for she fully understood the incomparable privations of a Southern soldier's life. She gave her gallant husband to the cause and her very last years in work for her beloved Confederate veterans.

> "A daughter of the Confederacy.
> One thought upholds her courage
> In storm and stress and gloom—
> She will not fail or trifle,
> Will bravely play her part;
> Because she knows a hero's blood
> Is beating in her heart."

The following incident of a woman of the Sixties in Lexington is narrated by Miss Camille Holt Hunt, whose mother, Francis Holt (Mrs. C. A. Hunt), whiled away many hours for her children with tales of her childhood in the Confederacy.

"My grandmother, Louisa Hogan, wife of Dr. William R. Holt, and her daughters, Claudia, Frances (my mother), and

Amelia, lived at the Homestead in Lexington, during the days of the Sixties. Four sons [had] gone to the front, all of whom died during the period of the war.

"My grandfather, although a practicing physician, owned a large plantation at Linwood, seven miles from Lexington, where he had spent much of his time in order to save what he could from raiders of all sorts, as he owned much cotton, stock, and fine mules. Therefore my grandmother and her three daughters were without male protection save for the faithful slaves.

"The days of 1861–65, when this section lived in constant fear of the coming of the Yankees and the depredations they might commit, were anxious ones for all Southern women, especially in 1865, when things were more lawless than ever.

"Finally the day arrived when Gen. Kilpatrick and his men did arrive in Lexington. The women in town, previous to this, made a raid on all places where whiskey was kept and poured it out, and all valuables were hidden. As was the custom of these men on their march, they demanded the best houses for their use, service, and whatever they cared to take. My grandmother, realizing how unprotected she and her daughters would be, used much wisdom and good judgment in the manner with which she managed the situation.

"She dispatched her faithful butler, 'Jerry,' with a note to Gen. Kilpatrick when he reached the suburbs of town, extending to him and his staff an invitation to be the guests of Mrs. W. R. Holt, at her residence the Homestead, while in town. This surprised the General, but [he] came to the front door where my grandmother met him with a courtesy [curtsy].

"The general, recognizing that he was in the presence of a lady to the manner born, accepted the hospitality offered with deference and respect and assured her that she and her family would be treated with consideration. Other homes were much abused and the owners suffered indignities.

"The Homestead at this time was the handsomest place in town, standing a hundred feet from the street amidst stately elm trees, occupying several acres. This was made the general's headquarters. In relating this my grandmother said that her blood boiled within her when she talked with the general, and the girls were weeping with anger and rebellion upstairs, but she knew they were helpless, and for the safety of her young daughters, pride had to be put aside.

"A United States flag was placed at the gate, and a guard carrying a gun paced back and forth in front of the house day and night. Traces of the path he made over the greensward remained there for many months.

"My grandmother and the girls occupied two bedrooms, on the door facings of which are still the iron receptacles for holding the bars across the doors. The girls ate their meals in their room, for they were very rebellious, and would not speak to them (the Yankees), especially the youngest, sixteen years of age. But my grandmother took her place at the head of the table, thus demanding order and respect at her board.

"As was usual, the kitchen, a large structure, was situated fifty feet from the 'big' house, and many outbuildings were scattered over the place. Maria and Betsy hated to cook for the Yankees at first, but liberal tips overcame this to some extent. One day the general asked if his French chef, who was with him, could go to the kitchen and prepare some of the food; this was permitted and he served many tempting dishes, none of which the girls would touch. [The Yankees] had the best of everything; of course sugar and coffee were scarce in those days but they had plenty of both, loaf sugar in twenty-five-pound blocks. My grandmother saved one of these until her oldest daughter was married, and her wedding cakes were made of it.

"One of the staff had a large trunk in his room filled with beautiful ladies' wearing apparel and silver which belonged to a lady in South Carolina, which he had confiscated. These he showed to the maids Thenie and Mandy, who told the girls.

"In their private conversation, many tales were told of what they [had] done in other places on their march, which convinced my grandmother that the only thing to do was to treat them as though she believed them to be gentlemen, and thus demand their respect.

"They had many fine horses, which delighted Kas, the coachman, and he wanted his mistress to accept a pair of these for the carriage, but she would not, but when they left the general presented Aunt Amelia with a beautiful black pony which she finally accepted and called 'Kilpatrick.' They had fine game chickens, and would go to the far end of the place and indulge in cock fighting, which would please the darkies.

"When the general took his departure he was most profuse in his thanks, and left some gold for my grandmother, which was about all they had except land to weather through the Reconstruction period."

YOUNG WOMEN TAKE MEN'S PLACES

"Dixie land of the long ago, from your flower-bordered pathway we gather these blossoms of history to weave a chaplet of glory to crown the girl heroes of the South in the Sixties."

After awhile when every male, both old men and young boys, [went] in the defense of their homes, the young women were taken in at the military posts, to do the work that a young man might do (as a stenographer of the present day). Early in 1864 the positions as clerk or copyists were offered to four young gentlewomen, Misses [Alice and Mary] Campbell, Stedman, Taylor, and Ellison, at the Fayetteville arsenal. The officials at the arsenal treated the young women clerks as honored guests, which the latter greatly appreciated. They remained there 'til Sherman's army, in March '65, destroyed every building on the arsenal grounds. As there was no money, the pay given these young ladies was black alpaca, which was kept in the arsenal to use in some way in making cartridges. The alpaca, combined with scraps of colored silk, made most elaborate dresses for these girls.

After the burning of her home by the Yankees in Washington, N. C., Miss E. M. B. Hoyt offered her services as clerk in the Commissary Department, at Granville, under Maj. De Meille, her brother-in-law. Her pay for faithful and efficient service was in tobacco, which was sold for twelve dollars in greenbacks.

Miss Anna Johnson, of Sampson County, enlisted as clerk at Brigade Headquarters in February '63 and served most efficiently.

Another young woman whom North Carolina claims, who took a man's place in the service of the Confederate government, was Miss Isabell Gill. Miss Gill served in the Confederate Treasury Department, and her signature is on many of the Confederate bills, which are now treasured relics. Her quick intelligence and fitness made her a valuable worker and her service was highly commended by the Confederate authorities.

The Children's Chapter of the Daughters of the Confederacy at Newton, North Carolina, is named in honor of this young woman, who at the close of the war married a Confederate soldier of that town, Sidney Wilfong, one of four brothers in the Confederacy.

RECOLLECTIONS OF YOUNG GIRLS

*"I wish I was in Dixie, away, away.
In Dixie's land I'll take my stand,
To live and die in Dixie."*

Some of the younger women kept diaries during the Sixties, and that kept by Miss Mary Ashe is a noteworthy record of the life of a young girl during these terrible four years. This girl of nineteen (when the war began) was one whom those who knew her put almost on a pedestal, and her diary shows her personal emotions with her prayers. It deserves preservation as indicating life among North Carolinians at this period, and is illustrative that North Carolina women presented an example never surpassed. Miss Ashe tells of her first war days spent in the country, at Rocky Point, near Wilmington, with her invalid mother and young sister (herself a delicate girl). Her father, the Hon. William S. Ashe, in the Confederate service at Richmond, having charge of the important duties of army transportation from the Mississippi river to Virginia—one brother, Maj. John Grange, at first with General Bragg at Mobile and then in Lee's army, and the other (Capt. Samuel Ashe), our State's distinguished historian, also in active service of the Confederacy. The first sorrow mentioned in this interesting diary was the tragic death of her father, from a railroad accident, [in] September, '62. At this time the diary records the imprisonment in Washington City of the brother

Samuel. After a hard winter the next grief recorded is the death of the invalid mother. Miss Ashe tells how the good God provided for her and her little sisters, and at length when her brother Samuel was ordered from the front (unsought by him) to the position of assistant to the commanding officer at the Fayetteville arsenal. Here the brother made a home for his young sisters, who busied themselves in activities for their soldier boys, with the other ladies of the town.

Though the handwriting is dim with years, yet this little diary of Mary Porter Ashe's contain a story duplicated among many of our women from '61 to '65, and it is a memorial to this lovely young girl whose life was cut off toward the close of the war.

> "Old times there are not forgotten:
> Look away! Look away! [Look away!] Dixie Land."

The following is written by Miss Kate McKimmon, for many years the honored and beloved "mother" of the girls at St. Mary's School, Raleigh, and a devoted lover of the Confederacy.

"The first five years of the Sixties found me as I still am, an un[re]constructed rebel! As a school girl at St. Mary's, I enjoyed marching with our 'crowd,' when with paper caps, Confederate flag, and a drum we paraded around the grove. In '61 on Saturday in the early spring the 'crowd' was proud to go to the Capitol to help the ladies who were making 'fatigue' suits for Manly's Battery. Some of us would run down to the 'Tuckers' or 'McKimmon's' for thread, needles, and material, gray flannel for the suits. Others would carry messages and materials from room to room. Well do I remember the day the Battery, of which my brother was a member, came to salute Gov. Ellis, before leaving Raleigh to join Lee's army in Virginia. Four years of honorable, courageous service that battery gave the Confederacy, standing by our Chieftain's side until he gave the command to surrender.

"St. Mary's School has a proud war record! Her doors were never closed to the request for help from those who, as 'The War' waged its relentless course were deprived of their homes; among those who asked for a home during the sad days was the family of Jefferson Davis, the beloved president of the Confederacy. The 'East Rock,' as known to St. Mary's girls, furnished a refuge to Mrs. Davis and four children, during the summer of '63. The beloved founder, Dr. Albert Smedes, educated many girls during these years whose fathers, being short of cash, brought their tuition in the form of provisions.

"When in '65, Johnson's army passed through Raleigh footsore, ragged, hungry, tradition has it that St. Mary's girls carried their dinner out to the gate and gave it to them. Well do I remember the day, April 12, '65. Throughout Raleigh, all along their march, food and water were carried to them. The appearance of that brave body of men, emaciated from lack of food and clothing, did not tend to produce any enjoyment in seeing the Yankee army, fat, sleek, with banners flying, drums beating, pass through our city, three days being required to accomplish it. 'Tecumseh Billie,' alias Gen. Sherman, pitched his tent in what was then the 'Governor's Palace.' My home was diagonally across the street, hence I had the pleasure of seeing many more 'blue-coats' than I desired. At night, I was often awakened by strains of beautiful music, for a moment I would enjoy the music of silver instruments, but when I would realize the instruments were 'Yankee,' I would 'cover up' and try not to hear.

"Raleigh was surrendered to Gen. Sherman on his entrance to the city, hence I am glad to say there was no robbing or sacking. As to the 'reconstruction' period, I leave its description to abler pens than mine. North Carolina was, I am glad to say, more fortunate than some of her sister States, South Carolina and Louisiana for example, but insults and indignities, to a greater or less extent, were heaped upon all who gloried in our beloved Southland."

Written by a devoted woman of the South, who as a young girl, was eyewitness to what she has written.

Though we are recording the part that the women and young girls took in the Confederacy, yet in almost every town of the State the boys were too young to be accepted for service, these youngsters gave real assistance to the women. We have mentioned the part taken by two of these "boys," Benehan Cameron and Francis Winston, and now we will give a few of the recollections of another "little boy of the Sixties." He is now North Carolina's valued historian (who has done so much to preserve our Confederate history), Col. F. A. Olds, collector of the State's Hall of History, Raleigh.

"The little boy of 1861–65, who writes these reminiscences now, used to go to Sunday School during the War between the States. There were no 'lessons' as they have now, and the churches were small. It was a sad time but few people were mourning, except in the large places. There were colporteurs, who took 'tracts' and Bibles to the soldiers in the camps. The writer now has a lot of the tracts, printed by the Confederate Bible Society.

"Sometimes soldiers came into the little schools and made talks to the youngsters. The writer was studying that then wonderful text book *The Scholar's Companion*, and McGuffey's Readers. Recitations were extremely popular then, and the girls were always, or nearly so, cleverer than the boys.

"We youngsters had a great admiration for the 'patrollers,' as the negroes always called the 'patrols' of citizens who kept order. There was a darky song, 'Run, nigger, run, de patroller'l ketch you; run, nigger, run, it's almost day.'

"New Year's Day was also a great occasion in those days. 'People of quality' kept open houses. There were streams of callers, all gentlemen, young and old, and the ladies were 'At Home' to them. There was 'eggnog' in the hall and a collation in the dining room. People had good appetites in those days and the hospitality was most generous and real. There was no 'paint and powder,' no 'make-up,' but everything was hearty and natural. It is a joy to have lived in those days, when there was no dope, cigarettes, 'gas,' or wild hurry to crowd 'a lifetime in a week.'

"The main street of Salisbury has quite a slope and one wet night as the mother of the writer was bringing him along on this street a courier dashed up on a big horse. He was a little fellow, just a boy, and as he pulled up his horse the latter stumbled and threw him. The lad fell on his head and his brains were exposed as he lay in a few yards of us.

"The 'refugees,' who had lived in the eastern counties of the State, and who fled when the Federal troops occupied the zone northward from New Bern, were also objects of interest. The up-country was strange to not a few of them, as very few people traveled in those days. They brought their slaves with them, unless the latter had 'run away.' In those days Raleigh and Hillsboro were considered by the coastal-plain folks to be 'up-country.'

"Thrift and infinitely careful saving were seen on all sides.

To waste was a sin in that trying time of war, and also before the war and after it. With 1,000,000 soldiers to clothe and feed, with no end of other pressing necessities to be met, every white and every black worked, worked, and worked. North Carolina had a fifth of all the 600,000 Confederate soldiers (from thirteen States) and hers were the best looked after. Besides this North Carolina was to an immense extent a furnisher of supplies to the rest of the Confederate armies. The state hummed like a beehive."

FIRST CONFEDERATE FLAGS MADE BY NORTH CAROLINA WOMEN

OUR DIVISION SONG
"There's a banner we uphold,
A banner without stain;
And in each precious fold,
We can see the past again,
Oh, the gallant hosts It lead,
Have become our glory dead,
But the stars and bars will live forever."
(Anna Jones Wooten)

When the North Carolina regiments marched off to war in the Confederate army, each regiment was required to have the regulation Confederate and North Carolina flags, both of which were furnished by the State. In many communities the women with loving hands made, with artistic embroidery, special flags for their regiments, and quite a little ceremony of presentation took place as the boys in gray marched off so gallantly.

A very few descriptions of these "presentation flags" have been secured, though many more communities than are recorded gave flags to their special regiments.

The names of Mrs. Rebecca Winborne and Maj. Orren Randolph Smith (Louisburg, North Carolina) are inseparably linked with the Southern Confederacy, from the fact that Capt. Smith designed and Mrs. Winborne made the first Confederate flag, the "Stars and Bars." After completing the design for the flag, after the Confederate Congress had advertised for models, Capt. Smith went to his friend (then Miss Rebecca Murphy, later Mrs. [Benjamin?] Winborne), and she put together and stitched the pieces for the flag. This was sent to Montgomery and accepted by the Confederate Congress as the official flag of the Confederacy in 1861. Mrs. Winborne also made a larger flag, nine by twelve feet, which was sent aloft on March 18th, 1861, on the Court House square at Louisburg, N.C., two months before North Carolina seceded.

The description of the flag as told by Mr. Smith is as follows:

"The idea of my flag I took from the Trinity—Three-in-One. The three bars were the Church, State, and Press. Red represented State, Legislative, Judiciary, and Executive; White for Church, Father, Son, and Holy Ghost; Red for Press, Freedom of Speech, Freedom of Conscience, Liberty of Press, all bound together by a field of blue, the heavens over all, bearing a star for each State in the Confederacy. The seven white stars, all the same size, were placed in a circle, showing that each State had equal rights and privileges, irrespective of size or population. The circle, having neither head nor foot, signified 'You defend me, and I'll protect you.'"

All claims and proof of these claims have been laid before a committee of the four Confederate organizations and all four have decided that to Orren Randolph Smith of North Carolina belongs the honor of having designed the Stars and Bars, [the] first Confederate flag. A beautiful marble fountain has been erected by the North Carolina Division, U.D.C. in

Louisburg, in memory of the designer of this flag, thus showing the appreciation the women of his State have for Orren Randolph Smith.

The North Carolina Division, U.D.C. has fittingly placed a monument at the grave of Mrs. Winborne in Wilson. The coming into existence of the Bonnie Blue Flag placed on a high place in the history of the Lost Cause the name of this lovely Southern woman, who proudly and lovingly constructed the flag under which Lee and Jackson led our splendid soldiers to battle.

The ladies of Louisburg can probably enjoy the honor of having made the first public presentation of the "Stars and Bars" to a military company. It was presented to the Franklin Rifles, in April, 1861, before North Carolina seceded, and Mr. J. E. Malone, of Laurinburg, has the paper containing the speech made by Miss Ella Nobles, and the one of acceptance by Capt. W. F. Green, also one by the Ensign, W. K. Barham. The old flag is in the Hall of History in Raleigh.

Gen. W. A Smith, commander of the North Carolina Division, U. C. V., tells us that in Ansonville, on February 2nd, 1861, a Secession flag was flung to the breeze, in large letters at the top was the word "Secession," while underneath was this motto: "Resistance to oppression is obedience to God." The flag was six by nine feet and attached to a long pole. Several young men of the village had made this flag of calico. The next day they carried it to the residence of Mrs. Garrett, "an enthusiast in the cause of secession," who, assisted by the young ladies, made a large flag of bunting, a duplicate of the calico flag. This flag was unfurled on the afternoon of February 3rd, '61; Misses Kate Smith and Winnie Watson made four rosettes and pinned them on the lapels of the young men who made the first flag, which, said one of them, "made us very proud and we walked the streets as vain as peacocks." Under cover of darkness, this first secession flag of bunting was cut down and destroyed, but these dauntless women made another larger and of finer material. No further attempts were made against it when hung. When the "Anson Grands" [i.e., Anson Guards], the first company in the State to offer its services to Gov. Ellis, left for the front, this secession flag was given to John Waddell to be presented to Gov. Ellis.

The women of Wadesboro made a silk flag for the Anson Guards as they left for war. It was of white with letters of blue, the silk being bought at Mr. Stacy's store, the letters being cut by Mrs. Lem Beeman. This flag (now in the Hall of History) was presented to the Anson Guards in April, '61, by Mrs. Hampton B. Hammond in behalf of the ladies and was received by Capt. Risden Tyler Bennett (later a colonel at twenty-one), the father of Mrs. Eugene Little, ex-president of this Division.

One of the oldest Confederate flags in our Hall of History was made and embroidered by Miss Christine Fisher, of Salisbury, made from a blue China crepe ladies' shawl, with the seal of North Carolina in high relief in the center. It was presented to her brother's (Col. Fisher's) regiment, and embroidered on it was "Sixth Infantry State Troops" with the regimental motto (chosen by Col. Fisher) "Do or Die." On the reverse side was "May 20th, 1775," date of the Mecklenburg Declaration.

The young ladies of Salisbury also made a silk flag for the Rowan Artillery, and it was presented to the departing soldiers by Miss Martha Marorie.

The first flag made in Washington was by Mrs. F. C. Roberts and Miss Manly—a silk flag the length of the room, for Fort Macon, a work of art, embroidered on it being a rattlesnake around a pine tree, the old State flag.

A beautiful flag was made for the Buncombe Riflemen by the following young ladies of Asheville: Misses Woodfin, Patton, Gaines, and Smith, Miss Anna Woodfin being chosen to present it. The material of the flag was contributed from the silk dresses of these young ladies. The "Riflemen" being the color company of the regiment in the battle of Bethel, this flag was the first one baptized in blood during the war! Miss Woodfin afterwards wrought, on its white bar with blue silk, the word "Bethel." It now drapes the portrait of Henry Wyatt in the State Hall of History.

The women of Washington gave a beautiful silk flag to the "Washington Grays" as they took their departure for the war. The white stripe in the flag was part of the satin wedding gown of Mrs. Thomas Myers, a cherished treasure, but given for the Confederate Cause. The account reads, "In the presence of a large gathering of the townspeople Miss Clara Hoyt presented the flag with a very appropriate address, and displayed a warmth of manner, a graceful self-possession, and a patriotism of feeling that none but a Southern lady knows how to exhibit. The tenor of her address was such as to infuse an amount of ardor and zeal into the company. Added to this influence was the appearance of several young ladies dressed in white, while such insignia as was emblematic of each seceding State.

"Their countenances beamed with an expression calculated to thrill the hearts of all who were about to leave at their country's call." In the fall of 1860, a Confederate flag made by Mrs. Watters and other ladies was flung from the window on the Court House, after a speech of acceptance.

Mrs. Anna McNair led the women of Tarboro in making their first flag, all the stars being outlined with white star braid. This was presented to the "Edgecombe Guards," their first volunteers, by Miss Cornelia Crenshaw, in a charming little speech.

Under the direction of Mrs. Patrick Henry Winston, the women of Windsor, Bertie County (among them being Misses Outlaw and Webb), made a flag for Company C, 11th North Carolina Regiment, of which Lt. Col. Francis W. Byrd was an officer. The flag was carried in many desperate battles and encounters, badly torn by shot and shell, and tattered by wind and rain. Rough soldier hands patched it as far as they could and followed this precious emblem made by their sisters at home. When Lee surrendered, the flag was in possession of Company C, Col. Byrd having been killed at Rhemn's station. Capt. Edward Outlaw and others on the morning of the surrender took the flag and secreted it under his coat, and went in a small skirt of woods and after tearing out a square of it, they burned it, rather than it should fall in the hands of the enemy. This precious relic Capt. Outlaw kept until his death. He was buried in 1922, in the beautiful Episcopal Church yard at Windsor, dressed in his Confederate uniform, and pinned above his heart was the small rag torn from the old tattered flag.

When Shelby's first company, under the leadership of Capt. A. W. Burton, departed for the war they were presented with a handsome Confederate flag made by Miss Julia Durham, (later Mrs. Green) and several Shelby ladies.

The presentation speech was made by Miss Durham, who at the time was only fifteen years of age, and reveals the faith and courage with which the daughters of the South sent away their men to fight for the beloved cause. The speech which has been preserved through the years is as follows:

"We in the name of the ladies of Shelby present you this flag. It is to assure you of the deep interest we feel in this coming crisis. Regardless of Northern scoffing and Southern terrorism you have at last faced your destiny, and may the god of battle assist you to maintain the honor of the Old North State and defend those rights maintained by our forefathers on the 20th of May, 1775. We have adopted the flag of the Confederate States, whose interests are inseparable from our own, and for the purpose of expressing our heartfelt sympathy for, and cooperat[ing] with, our noble brothers of the Sunny South. These hands shall unfurl this banner to the breezes, and it shall never be lowered at the command of the hired minions of Lincoln. Our cause is just and God will be with us. May you who have sacrificed your greatest interests to come forward and seek eagerly to defend your country at every hazard, return back to your fond homes and kindred uninjured. We bid you God speed."

The first flag of Forsyth County was made for Company I, Capt. A. H. Belo. It was made by Misses Bettie and Laura Lemly, Nellie Belo, [and] Carrie and Mary Fries. It was made of red, white, and blue silk and was embroidered in all large letters, with yellow silk, on the white side, with the words "Liberty or Death." After the war, Col. Belo settled in Texas, which accounts for the fact that after his death his widow presented the flag to the Texas Room in the Confederate Museum at Richmond, Va. The second flag was made by the same young ladies. They could not get more silk like the first, so used white silk for the whole flag, embroidering it in blue silk with the verse,

> "Our country first our glory and our pride,
> Land of our hopes, land where our fathers died,
> When in the right we'll keep thy honor bright,
> When in the right we'll die to set thee right."

This flag was made for the company commanded by Capt. Rufus Wharton. It was carried into several battles, was concealed on the person of its captain at the fall of Plymouth, and was brought home when he was exchanged. It was presented to the Wachovia Historical Society of Winston-Salem, several years ago, by Mrs. Blythe, of Philadelphia.

Both of these flags were presented to the companies of the Forsyth Rifles by Miss Bettie Lemly (later Mrs. Blacknall Brooks, of Salem), being carried by Misses Laura Lemly (who never married) and Mary Fries (who married Rufus Lenoir Patterson). The ceremony took place at the corner of Main and Bank Streets, the young ladies standing on the steps leading to the entrance of what is now known as the Belo Home, then a private residence belonging to Capt. Belo's father. Miss Sarah E. Shaffuer remembers passing just at the time for the presentation of the first flag, and being touched and thrilled by the sight of Miss Lemly making the presentation speech to Capt. Belo and his company.

The last company from Duplin County was Company E, 20th North Carolina, commanded by Capt. Denem [i.e., C. B. Denson], afterward sent to Virginia with Lewis T. Hicks as captain. As soon as this company was formed and ready to leave, Miss Rachale [i.e., Rachael] McIver presented it with a handsome flag, which she made herself. This flag was taken by him to Virginia and carried through the war, in many battles. It was highly appreciated by this company.

A flag was made by the young ladies of the Wayne County Female Academy for the Goldsboro Rifles and presented in April, '61 to the company's commander by Capt. M. D. Craten at Fort Macon. This flag was the only one laid upon the casket of Jefferson Davis at New Orleans. It is now on exhibition in our State Hall of History in Raleigh presented by the survivors of the Goldsboro Rifles.

The flag that was used at the funeral of Gov. Ellis in June 1861 had its motto, "Deeds, Not Words," embroidered on it; this is also one of the precious relics in the Hall of History.

Another flag in this collection is that made by Mrs. W. T. Southerland and presented to her husband's company, the "Milton Blues," of Cashwell [i.e., Caswell] County, in May, '61. It is made of heavy silk embroidered with eleven stars and the motto, "On to Victory."

A handsome flag was made by the women of Fayetteville for the Bethel Regiment, composed of the boys of the historic

Fayetteville Independent Light Infantry and the LaFayette Company, who were in the first North Carolina regiment. This was presented to them September 9th, '61, and was embroidered with the word "Bethel."

A beautiful silk flag was presented to the 1st North Carolina Cavalry, commanded by (afterwards General) Robert Ransom, from his devoted wife. With her own hand she embroidered a flag and presented it to the regiment just before it left for Richmond to be reviewed by President Davis. She requested that the flag never be surrendered, and after the fall at Appomattox, one of the men wrote, they never surrendered it, but sank it in the river. A newspaper clipping of this presentation is filed with Gen. Ransom's things in the Hall of History.

A handsome silk flag was made by Mrs. Elizabeth Slade Wiggins for the company which was organized by her husband, Mason L. Wiggins, in Halifax County several days before North Carolina seceded. This mother of seven sons in the Confederacy (herself of patriotic revolutionary stock) was ardent in her love for the Confederacy, and her home, Woodlawn, was the mecca for the sick soldiers who came through Halifax. Her diary, kept all during the war, is filled with many interesting facts and bits of history of that period that will bear preserving.

In her sketch of Company I, 6th North Carolina Regiment, Mrs. A. J. Ellis, the beloved historian of the Raleigh "Daughters," tells of the presentation of a beautiful flag to these boys of the Morrisville and Cedar Fork communities of Wake County. She says, "A beautiful banner of blue silk, trimmed with white silk fringe, the North Carolina coat of arms painted in one corner, and the inscription, "To the Morrisville Grays by the Ladies of Cedar Fork," in the center, had been made by Misses Morris, Page, and Lyon. This was presented to the company by Miss Jennie Lyon in an appropriate address, being accepted by Lt. Page. After patriotic songs and resounding cheers by the soldiers, a Bible was given each man by the ladies. The flag was captured during the war by Maj. Wiggins, of Ohio, and a great celebration took place at Cedar Fork when it was received by the lady who first presented it, now Mrs. [Fannie Lyon] Lowe. This flag is now in the Hall of History in Raleigh.

> "The Stars and Bars are furled, but loved the same,
> And through the bloody stains we love the name
> Of Stars and Stripes, for which we fight today,
> The old flag is not lost, but laid away,
> So do not say, FORGET!"

Flags Presented by the Charlotte Women

Charlotte was not behind the other communities in presenting flags to her military companies, the "Hornet's Nest" and the "Charlotte Grays," as they left for the war.

Mrs. J. A. Fore, former historian of the North Carolina Division, has given this very interesting account of the presentation ceremonies of these flags.

"The 'Hornet's Nest Riflemen' were organized many years before the War between the States, and was one of the first companies to volunteer and be mustered into the service of the State.

"A beautiful Confederate flag was presented to the 'Hornets' by the young ladies of Charlotte, on the 18th of April, 1861, and the presentation speech was made by Miss Sadler. The account is published in *The Daily Bulletin*, April 20th, 1861. The last clause of her speech reads thus—'The prayers, the hopes, the hearts of our ladies go with you. We feel that success will crown our banner. We have no room for fears. To God and our community we devote you.'

"The account says further that the Hornet's Nest Riflemen were ordered to Wilmington to assist in taking possession of the ports, so as to anticipate Lincoln's action and to prevent bloodshed.

"The captain of the company was L. S. Williams, father of Mrs. J. P. Caldwell.

"The 'Charlotte Grays' was a company of boys under twenty-one years of age, and the captain was young Edgar Ross, who was only nineteen years of age. The presentation of the beautiful hand-painted banner took place in the Presbyterian church yard, and the speech was made by Miss Hattie Howell, a beautiful young girl of sixteen years, who said: 'Capt. Ross, I present to you this flag for the Charlotte Grays, knowing that whatever happens it will never, while a man of you lives, be lowered in disgrace.' Capt. Ross responded thus: 'Miss Howell, and young ladies of Charlotte, we are honored by your gift. We accept this flag with thanks, and promise you, in the name of this company, that the Charlotte Grays will never see it dishonored. We may die in its defense, but dishonored it shall never be.'

"This company and the Hornet's Nest Riflemen both were in the First Bethel Regiment, commanded by Col. D. H. Hill, afterward General, that fought the first battle of the war, and caused it to [be] said that 'North Carolina was first at Bethel, etc.'"

FIRST MONUMENTS AND MEMORIAL ASSOCIATIONS BY THE WOMEN OF NORTH CAROLINA

> "Then tell it, tell the story
> Carve it in living stone!
> Proclaim it to ages hoary,
> The Southland enshrines her own."

Probably the first monument erected by any band of Southern women (the forerunner of many others) was over the grave of Miss Anne Carter Lee, by the women of Warren County; just before the war closed. Miss Lee, the daughter of Gen. Robrt E. Lee, had died in the summer of '62, while refugeeing with her mother at Jones's Sulphur Springs, and was buried in the Jones's burial grounds. The committee was composed of the following women with Mrs. Joseph Speed Jones as chairman: Mrs. Wharton Green (who made the first contribution of two hundred dollars), Mrs. Lucinda Jones, and Misses Maria Alston, Heck, and Brownlaw. These women sacrificed the remnant of their jewels and made other self-denials to thus honor the memory of the daughter of the South's Chieftain! Not a man was asked to contribute a cent.

Warren County, like many other parts of the State, was the home of loyal Confederate women, among them being Mrs. Wharton Green, who (when Col. Green was away) sold her diamonds and bought ammunition and uniforms for his company. Mrs. Lucy Polk (née Williams), said to be the greatest belle the State has ever produced, gave of her means and services to the Cause, encouraging many a soldier by her loveliness of character. Another was Mrs. Joseph Jones, whose deeds of kindness to Confederate widows were innumerable.

Women of Fayetteville Erect First Confederate Monument in North Carolina.

Early Memorial Association

"Southern monuments are love tokens, of wounded hearts; emblems of tenderness and grief, of a mighty sorrow that is incurable."

A few days after Sherman's raid through Fayetteville, Mrs. Jesse (Anne K.) Kyle, with other ladies, secured from the mayor the back part of the cemetery, overlooking Cross Creek. The eighteen soldiers who had already died in the hospitals there and were interred in a lot on the creek, were disinterred and buried with twelve others in this lovely spot, by historic Cross Creek. Foot stones were placed at each grave and the names marked on them. Just at sunset Rev. Joseph C. Huske read the words "I am the Resurrection and the Life," while the caskets were lowered to their last resting place. A few girls of Fayetteville met daily under the direction of Mrs. Maria Spear at the home of the Misses [Carrie and Maggie] Mallett, the first meeting being with Mrs. Jesse Kyle, and from bits of brightened scraps of their dresses made a handsome silk quilt. This was sold at a dollar a share and the sum of three hundred dollars was raised, with which a marble monument was bought. This shaft was erected December 30th, 1868, over thirty graves whose occupants died in our hospitals. It was the first Confederate Monument in North Carolina and one of the first in the South. The ladies sent the quilt to President Davis, and it is now in the North Carolina room at Richmond. During the time of the making of the quilt a few ladies of Fayetteville, the first ones being Mrs. Kyle [and] Misses Mallett, [Maggie] Anderson, [Alice and Mary] Campbell, [Kate] McLaurin, and [Alice] Poe, would gather quietly in the early morning and decorate the graves of the soldiers, one of them reading a prayer. This was the beginning of the Memorial Association of Fayetteville (now the U.D.C.), which has never failed in all these years to perpetuate this loving and sacred custom. For many years every tenth of May (our Memorial Day) the exercises have been held around this hallowed spot by old Cross Creek, while they "cover them over with beautiful flowers and deck them with garlands, these heroes of ours."

Memorial Association of Wilmington

On July 20, 1866, the women of Wilmington met at the City Hall, where they made plans for the first decoration of their soldiers' graves after the war. At this meeting Mrs. Armand DeRosset, who had been president of the Soldiers' Aid Society (organized May, 1861), proposed a permanent memorial association. Her suggestion found an echo in the hearts of all present, and then and there the "Ladies Memorial Association of Wilmington" was formed. At that time the city being under martial law, word was sent to Washington that the "rebel women of Wilmington were plotting treason." The authorities wired [the] Federal officer in command of

Wilmington, "What are the rebel women of Wilmington doing?"

His response that the ladies of Wilmington were "quietly at their homes" won for him the gratitude of the "rebel women."

In 1867 the association was presented with a beautiful plot at Oakwood [i.e., Oakdale] Cemetery. The last interment in this memorial plot was that of an unknown soldier killed while the Federal gunboats were coming up the Cape Fear River in 1865, and buried by the roadside where he had fallen. His body was reinterred beside these other heroes by the women of Wilmington.

The monument to their Confederate dead was erected by this memorial association in 1872, the bronze used in this being made from cannon captured during the war.

"No nation, people, race—in any way—so many monuments have reared as we the Southrons; every modest town may see stones of remembrance to the Men in Gray."

The history of the Ladies Memorial Association of Wake County is one of the most notable of this State, and shows the unfaltering spirit of these women. Mrs. Armistead Jones, a daughter of the gallant Gen. Branch, has written at our request a most interesting and accurate history of this, one of the first associations to be organized in North Carolina. From her records we find that soon after the State Capitol was taken possession of by the Yankees (in '65), the mayor was notified that the bodies of the Confederate soldiers who had died in the hospitals in Raleigh and [been] buried there must be removed so that their dead might be buried on this spot. A few of the ladies who had worked in the soldiers' hospitals and sewing societies then organized themselves into this memorial association, the following being the charter members: Mrs. L. O'B. Branch (widow of Gen. Branch), president; Mrs. Henry Miller, vice-president; Miss Sophia Partridge, secretary; Miss Anne Mason Leeds, Mrs. John Devereux, and Miss Margaret Iredell. On receiving an order that unless the remains of the Confederates were removed at once they would be thrown out in the road, these women, accompanied by some of the gentlemen of Raleigh, with shovels and wheelbarrows tenderly and carefully reinterred them in another spot, making with their own hands the rough hewn coffins. A plot of ground was given the ladies by Mr. Henry Mordecai; also one was offered by Miss Anne Devereux, stipulating in the deed that no one but a Confederate soldier could be buried there. Some time later the ladies had 108 bodies of their soldiers removed from Arlington and interred in this beautiful Confederate Cemetery, where now are laid to rest those from the Soldier's Home as they "pass over the river." Soon after this, a monument was erected there.

Women of New Bern Organize Memorial Association

After suffering so much during the war, the women of New Bern were among the first to organize a memorial association, the object being to care for their dead heroes. Mrs. F. C. Roberts (until recently the oldest living member of the twenty-two women who were charter members, with Mrs. B. C. Davis as president), in her history of this association, says: "In an open field at the edge of town, there were many graves marked with wooden strips, which were already decaying. Yankees and Confederates had been buried together. The U.S. army, then in power, had appropriated a spacious plot for their dead and were removing them and beautifying their resting place. The enemy generously offered to provide coffins, and bury our dead also. We declined the offer, particularly as their coffins were regulation length, and if one poor fellow happened to be a little too tall, they jumped on him and mashed him down. We got permission from our rulers (it was in Reconstruction days, we were under martial law) to allow our graves to remain unmolested till we were ready to care for them. Oh! We were so poor and so desperate these days; but our hearts were filled with patriotic zeal that could remove mountains and defy all obstacles. It required patience, hard work, and rigid self-denial to raise three thousand dollars with which to build our monument. This we accomplished in many efforts. A bazaar brought us in one thousand dollars. Tableaux and concerts and private contributions completed the sum, but this took time."

The women of Tarboro began their memorial association early after the war, led by Mrs. Henry Dockery and Miss Arabella Clark Parker, who were devout in their ministrations for the dead, as they had been to the living soldiers.

Monument at Battlefield of Averasboro by Community Women.

The following account of the Memorial Society of the women of the Averasboro community, probably one of the first in the South, is given by Miss Jessie Slocumb Smith, the president of the Dunn Chapter U.D.C.

"Soon after the close of the war, the neighbors in the vicinity of the battle of Averasboro disinterred these bodies of our Confederate dead and removed them to an appropriate spot near the third line of breastworks. This spot they named Chicora. Very appropriate the name seems, as Chicora is the Indian name for Carolina, and most of the dead were South Carolinians, whose bodies and memories have been carefully cherished by this North Carolina community.

"To the John Smith home mentioned before, Oak Grove it was called, there came also the proud honor of receiving the first, or one of the first memorial associations organized in the South. The ladies of the neighborhood had during the year '66 formed an organization and decorated the graves in that spring, and now the ex-Confederate hospital, again occupied by its former owners, opened its doors with gracious hospitality to receive the ladies, who on May 15th, 1867, formally organized the Smithville Memorial Association 'for the purpose of procuring funds for enclosing the cemetery, and for erecting a monument to the memory of our Confederate dead who fell in the battle of Averasboro, N.C.'

"The old organization was sustained and the following officers elected: president, Mrs. Julia J. Williams; vice-president, Mrs. R. R. Roberson; vice-president, Miss Bertie Sanders; vice-president, Miss Sallie Smith; vice-president, Miss S. E. Smith; secretary, Miss Louise Smith; treasurer, Miss Janie Smith; corresponding secretary, Mrs. J. C. Smith.

"How diligently this memorial association labored is shown by the fact that as early as February 15th, 1868, a substantial iron railing was purchased for the cemetery. A monument, a handsome one for its time, was then erected, and unveiled May 10th, 1872. As to the work and sacrifice required to accomplish this, the following is copied from a letter written by the last surviving charter member of the association, one who has since gone to join those brave comrades of the Sixties: 'While this monument fittingly marks the resting place of loved and honored dead, fallen heroes of the Confederate army, yet it also memorializes the devotion, heroism, and nobility of soul of their survivors. In those days a dollar loomed large with importance, and each gift represented toil and sacrifice.' The work was begun just after our country had been devastated by the enemy, and was still garrisoned by Federal troops. Collection of funds was carried on during the period of reconstruction.

"Through all the sixty intervening years since those brave men so nobly gave their all, the same spirit of devotion to a righteous cause has kept alive the old memorial association. Not once has a Tenth of May rolled round that the cemetery has not been put in order and appropriate exercises held. And this the more remarkable as it was an isolated country neighborhood.

"On May 10th, 1904, the Smithville Memorial Association became the Chicora Chapter of the Daughters of the Confederacy of Dunn, N.C. Right bravely have the daughters carried on the work of the mother association. Could the organizers of the sixties look down, they could proudly say, 'Well done my daughters.'

"Oh Mothers of the Sixties! yours was a noble work, nobly done. The torch held so high and yet so bravely has been passed to our hands. Ours the task to hold it high, ours the task to pass it on. May we bear it in your same lofty spirit; may we carry on the work with your same unselfish devotion."

A story of real heroism lies behind the unique inscription on a tombstone, referred to on page 31. This inscription brings a vision of a woman unafraid, who fought for her home and the ham bone which was all she had left for the two convalescing soldier sons who had returned from camp after being wounded. The young woman was Mrs. Rebecca Jones [Alford], wife of G. H. Alford, a member of the Pleasant Grove Baptist Church of Wake County, whose son, the late George Benton Alford, erected this monument to his plucky mother.

Mrs. Alford not only charged with an unexpected fierceness that disarmed Sherman's soldiers from stealing her precious ham bone, but when one of them threatened to burn the negro quarters, she picked up a stick of wood and hit him over the head. This was truly a soldier without gun or sword, who kept her home intact.

NORTH CAROLINA MOTHERS OF MANY SONS

"The greatest battle that was ever fought,
Shall I tell you where and when?
On the maps of the world you'll find it not;
It was fought by the mothers of men."

The unfaltering courage of the Confederate women was especially shown when a mother sent forth a number of her sons in their young manhood "to do or die." We are here recording only a comparatively few names of such mothers, and feel that this is only the beginning of a splendid honor roll of our State's mothers of the War between the States.

The mother whose name deserves to stand foremost in this honor roll is Mrs. Lemuel (Lucy Faucett) Simpson, of Alamance County, who gave all her sons, ELEVEN, to the Confederacy. The names of these were: William, Faucette, Benjamin Franklin, Lemeul, George Washington, Jefferson, Martin Van Buren, James Ruffin, Haywood, Henry Jackson, and Wyatt.

Next we record eleven who volunteered within a week, the mother of these being Mrs. Reuben Jones (Flora Macdonald), of Scotland County, who seemed to inherit the brave and gallant spirit of her namesake, the Scotch heroine of Prince Charlie fame, who bravely said to her eleven boys, "I can not hold you, when your country calls you." The names of these sons were: Daniel, John, William, Archibald, James, Duncan, Hiram, [Malcolm], Sandy (or Alexander), Dougal, and Samuel. All of these are dead except Samuel, the youngest one.

Next on our honor roll we place the name of Mrs. Robert Tolar (Fannie Autry), of Cumberland County, who gave her husband, nine sons, one son-in-law, and her fifteen-year-old grandson, John R. Tolar. After heroically bidding good-bye to her husband and nine sons, Mrs. Tolar devoted herself to her large plantation, from which she supported many needy families of absent soldiers. The names of her nine sons are: Alfred, Haynes, Joseph, Matthew, Thomas, Sampson, William, John, and Robert.

Another mother of nine sons was Mrs. Robert Thomas (Mary Lewis), of Granville County.

Mrs. Nancy Stinson, of Chatham County, gave nine sons and enough relations to the Confederate cause to form a company. She gave her children, her love, her time, and her work, and she was known far and wide as Mother Stinson. She lived to the ripe old age of ninety-eight, being an honorary member of the Winnie Davis Chapter, U.D.C., at Pittsboro.

A mother of nine sons in the service of the Confederacy was Mrs. James (Sarah Goodman) Deaton, of Iredell County. These were Caleb, who lost his mind from brutal prison treatment, Thomas, Aaron, both killed in battle, John, Samuel, Edward, Cornelius, George, and Pinckney.

We find also the following names of mothers of eight sons in the Confederacy. Mrs. [Farquhard] Smith, of Averasboro (then Cumberland, now Harnett County), gave her eight sons to the Confederate service. One son, Alex, was in the home guard; Curtis and Farquhard were in the medical department; James, Douglas, and Henry were in the cavalry; and Edward was in the infantry. The youngest, Jesse Slocumb, a lad of sixteen, was a courier boy on the staff of Gen. Hardee in the battle of Bentonville, N.C. Mrs. Smith herself was the granddaughter of Colonel Ezekiel Smith and his wife, Mary Slocumb, the heroine of Moore's Creek battle. So this Confederate mother inherited her patriotism.

The widow Stephens, of Buncombe County, gave her all—her eight stalwart sons—to the Confederacy. The name of Mrs. Stephens of Buncombe County should hold a high place on the honor roll. She gave her eight sons, all farmers, to fight for their country, running the farm herself and fighting a real fight on her mountain farm. All of these eight boys returned to her, and forty-three years after their soldier life all the eight were living—a remarkable record. Joining the widow Stephen's farm were the Blacks, which family also gave eight members to the Confederacy, seven sons and the father. Sixteen soldiers from two families.

The widow Polly Ray of the Longstreet community,

Cumberland County, gave her seven sons, from the youth of sixteen to the son of thirty. None had greater anguish of heart than this poor widow, who was left when the war ended with only her young daughter, as all of her seven sons lost their lives on the battlefields of the Confederacy. In this whole neighborhood of Longstreet (one of the earliest Scotch settlements of the State), every young man volunteered for service at the first of the war, and so many were killed that it is said that there was not a birth in that community for many years.

Mrs. Olive Tatum, of Bladen County, gave seven sons to the Confederacy; five of these gave up their lives in the service—she was truly a "Mother of the Gracchi." The names of these were: Marshal, Richard, Jonathan, Simeon, Gray, Hanson, and Alexander. Only two of these returned.

Those who gave seven sons to the service are Mrs. Mason Lee Wiggins (Elizabeth Slade), of Woodlawn, Halifax County, their names being: William, Blake, John, Alfred, Thomas, Octavius, Eugene, the latter entering the army at fourteen years of age.

Another mother of seven sons was Mrs. Black of Buncombe County, who gave not only her sons but her husband to the Confederate service.

Mrs. Thomas (Rachael Jeffries) Moore, of Alamance County, gave her seven sons; they were: Harrison, Solomon, Evans, Isaac, Jefferson, William, and Haywood.

Old Mrs. Sally Michels, of Burke County, gave seven sons to the war, and the maker of the famous clay pipes, she kept many a soldier happy with her gifts which "went up in smoke." When Col. Wm. Pearson, of Morganton, after his return from Italy, told her that King Victor had pronounced her clay the best he'd ever smoked, "Aunt Sally" with a toss of her head said, "That's nothing, Zeb Vance said that it was the best he ever tried." "Aunt Sally" showed her State pride.

Mrs. David Stevenson, of Johnston County, gave seven sons and not one of them received a scratch.

Mrs. Jane Cooper Stratford, of Guilford County, gave seven sons for the army.

Mrs. Neal McLean, of Laurinburg, was another mother of seven sons—three being killed in battle.

Mrs. Alvi Robbins, who was Miss Mary Brown, of Randolph County, gave six sons to the war. These were: Julius Alexander, Franklin Childs, James LaFayette, Madison Columbus, Roswell Washington, and William McKindy. When the body of her fourth son was brought home from the battlefield, the mother of these six soldiers leaned over the casket with a face like marble, and said, "Though He slay me yet will I trust in Him."

Mrs. Thomas Morgan, of Granville County, gave six sons to the Confederacy, and *all six were killed in service*. Truly her name should be recorded in letters of gold.

There were six sons of Mrs. Henry G. (Elizabeth Arrington) Williams, of Granville County, who were in the service. They were: Col. Solomon (killed in action), Samuel, A. H. A., Thomas (killed), John, and William (died in service).

Mrs. Armand DeRosset (Eliza Lord), that splendid war mother of Wilmington, gave six sons, John, William, Louis, Armand, Thomas, and Edward, and three sons-in-law to her Southland.

Mrs. Able Bowden, of Franklin County, sent six sons to the war, five of these taking part in the battle of Fort Fisher.

Mrs. Robert (Margaret Robertson) Burwell, of Charlotte, gave six sons, who were: John Bott, Armistead, William Robertson, [Dandridge] Spottswood, Robert Turnbull, and James Webb. Robert and James lost their lives, the latter in his teens.

Mrs. Thomas Chandler, of Granville County, had six sons in the great struggle.

Six sons of Mrs. Richard Stallings, of Franklin County, were in the Confederate army, only one of them returning to her.

Mrs. Mary Morrow Heath (whose plantation joined the birthplace of Andrew Jackson in Union County) gave six sons to the service. This splendid mother of the Confederacy lived to be ninety-four, and these sons lived to be leaders in North Carolina's prominent business activities.

Mrs. William White (Sarah Wilson), of Charlotte, gave six splendid sons to the Confederate army.

Mrs. Samuel Mitcherson, of Wake County, was another mother of six sons in the Confederacy.

In the roll of mothers who gave six sons to the Confederacy is Mrs. Henry (Maria Edmundson) Best, whose sons were Robert, Henry, William E., T. H., B. J., and R. E.

Mrs. Alex Dixon, of Orange County, gave her six sons.

Mrs. Lewis Smith was the mother of six sons.

Mrs. Hudlah Padrick, and Mrs. Thomas Garman, of Onslow County, each gave six sons to the Confederacy.

Mrs. Jonathan M. Stone (Rebecca Jane) gave six sons for the Confederacy, from Nash County; they were: Albert, Silas, Rufus, Jackson, Atlas, and Marion.

Among the mothers of six sons in the war was Mrs. Daniel Seagle, of Lincoln County. Their names form an array of patriotic Americans, being: Thomas Jefferson, James Monroe,

Martin Van Buren, Polk Dallas, Benjamin Franklin, Nathaniel Macon, and Andrew Jackson [n.b.: seven names].

Mrs. John Wilfong, of Newton, was another mother of six sons in the war. These were: Milton, Henry, Pinkney, John, Sidney, and Charles. Besides these she gave (through her daughter) her son-in-law, Capt. M. L. McCorkle.

In the list of mothers who gave five sons to the service is Mrs. Thomas Carlton, of Burke County, every one of them being killed. When the news finally came that her blue-eyed, bright-haired baby boy, a lad just sixteen, had fallen, she called her son-in-law who had been discharged by the army surgeon as unfit for duty, and said, while trembling with emotion: "Get your knapsack, William, the ranks must be filled."

Such were the Spartan Mothers of the Confederacy.

It fell to Mrs. Morrison, of Davidson College (a sister of the ex-Governor Graham), to give not only her own five sons to the Confederacy, but four most distinguished sons-in-law in the war. The latter were: Stonewall Jackson, Gen. D. H. Hill, Gen. Barringer, and Maj. Avery, truly an Honor Roll of which the State was proud.

Mrs. Isaac Avery, of Morganton, an untiring worker for the Cause, gave five sons to the war, two of them never returning.

Mrs. Amos (Caroline Louisa Tomlinson) Weaver, of Iredell County, had five sons in the war; they were: George Washington, Henry Clay, Franklin Harrison, Romulus Lafayette, and Preston DeKalb.

Mrs. Allison Lee Watson, born Elizabeth Yarborough, of Lexington, had five sons serving in the Confederate army, four of these having made the supreme sacrifice, the last one who enlisted at sixteen being left to her. The names of these sons are: Albert, James, Archibald, Charles, and Haywood.

Mrs. William Joyner, of Franklin County, was the mother of five Confederate soldiers (two of them being twins), besides giving up her husband. *Four of her boys were in the battle of Gettysburg.*

Among the mothers who gave five sons was Mrs. Sarah Jones Gill, of Wilson. These were: Frank, Thomas, Benjamin, John, [and] James; two of them never returned.

Mrs. Sallie Lancaster Hargrove, of Moore County, gave five sons to the Cause of the South.

Mrs. Sophia Stedman[, of] Rutherfordton (a widow), sent five sons to the war, Townsend, John, William, Josh, and Joe.

Mrs. Zephaniah (Lucretia) Askew, of Hertford County, gave her five sons, Levi, Wilbur, Richard, Zephaniah, and Edward.

Mrs. Godwin Moore, of Hertford County, gave John, Julian, Thomas, James, and William.

Mrs. Mary Eliza Wooten, of Pitt County, sent five sons to the war: John, Edward, Lewis, Allen, [and] Oscar.

Mrs. David Ingle, of Alamance County, was another mother who gave five sons; they were: Sidney, Rufus, Albert, Mabin, and Thaddeus.

Mrs. Samuel T. Allston, of Warren County, had five sons, the youngest of whom, Philip, is now commander of the first brigade of the North Carolina Division, United Confederate Veterans.

Mrs. Elizabeth Hoke Rowe, of Cabarrus County, had five sons in the war, and Mrs. Katherine Fry Smyre, of the same county, also had five sons in service. These two women lived on and owned large adjoining farms, from which they sent large supplies to the army.

Mrs. Angus McCatten, of Moore County, had five sons to volunteer for the service, *all of them returning alive.*

Mrs. Edna Barnes, of Johnston County, gave five sons.

Mrs. Ashley Horne, of Johnston County, was the mother of five sons in the service of the Southland, three of them being killed in the war.

Mrs. Funifold (Kate Harrison) McDanial, of Trenton, had five sons in the cavalry, all of these taking their horses with them from their plantation.

Among the mothers of four sons in the Confederacy was Mrs. William R. (Louisa Hogan) Holt, of Lexington, all of whom made the "supreme sacrifice" in the war.

Mrs. John McRae (Mary Shackleford), of Fayetteville, gave four sons to the service. They were: James, Thomas, Robert, [and] John, and her stepson Duncan, making five McRaes from one family.

Mrs. Oran Allston Palmer, of Chatham County, gave her four sons, and *all four were killed at the battle of Gettysburg.*

Mrs. John Buxton Williams, of Warren County, gave four sons to the Confederacy: James, Harry, John, and Solomon. Her home, Buxton Place, was a home for all the soldiers passing through Warren County, and this warm-hearted woman filled their knapsacks as they departed with a cheery goodbye.

Mrs. Amos Weaver, of [Lenoir], gave up four sons; they were: Franklin, George Washington, Preston, and Rufus.

Mrs. Samuel Bennett (Jane Little), of Anson County, gave her four sons: John, Thomas, William, and Frank.

Mrs. William Pridgen (Patsy Lindsay), of Nash County, gave Alexander, Drewry, Josiah, and Henry to the cause.

Mrs. Fannie Browning Smith, of Union Ridge, sent four sons; the last, a mere boy being brought back to her a corpse, was Robert Lawson Smith.

Mrs. Lauchlan Bethune and Mrs. Flora Baker, of Moore County, each gave four sons.

Mrs. Frederick Battle (Tempie Perry), of Franklin and Nash Counties, gave four sons to the cause.

Mrs. (Rebecca Moore) Allen, wife of James J. Allen, gave four sons to the Confederacy: Andrew, Thomas, James, [and] William.

Mrs. May Ruffin and Mrs. Abia Person, of Franklin County, each gave four sons to the South.

Mrs. Duncan McGougan (Annie White) of Robeson County, gave four sons: Daniel, James, Alexander, and Reuben.

North Carolina's role of mothers of three sons in the Confederacy would fill a volume, but the few of such names that have been secured deserve to be recorded.

The only record we have of a mother who gave TRIPLETS to the Confederate army from North Carolina is that of Mrs. Margaret Smith Gibbs, of Wilkes County. The names of these triplets were: William, Thomas, and Robert.

Mrs. Sarah Williams Chance, wife of Tillman F. Chance, of Rockingham County, had three sons in the war: Andrew Jackson, William Anderson, [and] Tillman Franklin, Jr. The latter died in camp in October '62, leaving a little daughter whom he had never seen, this little girl now being Mrs. J. E. Heinzerling, of Statesville, historian of the chapter there.

Mrs. Mary (Laura King) Davidson, of Mecklenburg County, also contributed three sons to the Southern Cause; they were: John, Robert, and Richard.

Mrs. Celia D. Bason, of Alamance County, gave three sons to Lee's army; they were: James, George, and William.

Mrs. Charles Manly, the wife of [the e]x-Governor of North Carolina, gave three sons and three sons-in-law, two of whom were killed in battle.

Mrs. Tempe Boddie Yancey, of Warren County, gave her sons George, Henry, and John.

Mrs. Lucinda Walker, of Union Ridge, sent to war John, William, and Joshua.

Mrs. Andrew Grier (born Margaret, daughter of Gen. Paul Barringer), of Mecklenburg County, gave three sons; they were: Samuel, William, and Laban, besides her stepson, Thomas.

Mrs. Delany Andrews, of Asheboro, sent Allen, Thomas, and Hezekiah.

Mrs. Harriet Phillips gave her three sons, Joseph, James, and Frederick, of Tarboro.

Mrs. Martha Thorne Nichols, of Halifax County, gave three sons to the Confederacy.

Mrs. Edward McKethan, of Fayetteville, had three sons in the war, Hector, Augustus, and Edward.

Mrs. John Moore, of Pitt County, sent her three sons to the war: John, Albert, and William.

Mrs. Jacob (Elizabeth) Sharpe, of Hertford County, gave all her sons, Thomas, William, and Henry Clay.

Mrs. Henry A. London (Sallie Lord), of Wilmington and Pittsboro, gave her three boys, William Lord, Rufus Marsden, and Henry Armand.

The following women of Hertford County each gave three sons: Mrs. Sophia Taylor gave John, Dorsey, and Lafayette.

Mrs. Lewis Pruden had Charles, Henry, and John in the war.

Mrs. Harriett Deanes gave her three, James, John, and Jefferson.

Mrs. Carian Morris gave her sons, William, Calvin, [and] Alpheus.

Mrs. William (Emily) Joyner, of Pitt County, gave her three sons, Robert, John, and Edmund. The latter is the beloved Chaplain of the North Carolina Division, United Confederate Veterans.

Mrs. Lettie Jones Long, of Alamance County, gave her three sons to the Confederacy, *and all were killed*. They were:- Jacob, Thomas, and Robert. The fourth and youngest son ran away and reached the army as the surrender took place.

The story of how this widowed mother made a very dangerous journey to Virginia to find and bring back her wounded boy, going into the battlefield midst shot and shell, is one of real courage. The body of another son was brought back to this mother, *two months after he had been killed*. With devotion seldom equaled, Mrs. Long herself bathed and dressed the pitiful form of her loved one, saying that her boy should be cared for decently and tenderly, by his mother. *Such as this was the spirit of the Confederate mothers.*

Confederate Mother Now Living

North Carolina has the distinction of having a CONFEDERATE MOTHER NOW LIVING, who is nearing her one hundred and third birthday. This centenarian is Mrs. Julia Anne Pridgen, a resident of Pender County, who lives near the site of the famous revolutionary battle of Moore's Creek Bridge. Mrs. Pridgen was the mother of a Confederate soldier, M. B. Pridgen, now deceased, while her second son had volunteered to join the army when the war ended, he being too young before this. The reminiscences of this MOTHER OF THE CONFEDERACY are worthy of a volume by itself, as she vividly recalls not only the events of the War between the States but those of the Mexican outbreak. From her mental and physical strength it would not be surprising if Mrs. Pridgen should not add several years to the one hundred and three she has already lived.

All honor to this living MOTHER OF A CONFEDERATE SOLDIER!

WELCOME HOME, HEROES IN GRAY!

"I'm glad I am in Dixie, hooray, hooray.
In Dixie's land I'll take my stan,
To lib and die in Dixie."

As the men in gray, tattered, footsore, dispirited, returned to their desolate homes, their women quieted them with undimmed courage and sweet resolution, arousing them to manly endeavor. Hundreds of these delicate women, bred in affluence, were bravely working with their hands for their daily bread. Many in old age, alone in the world, were bereft of all their possessions.

These women had a difficult task to perform, and they nobly performed it! When the end came, instead of sitting down in despair, these women of the Confederacy led the way in building up the homes and shattered fortunes of the South.

It has been said that the Confederacy never would have lasted for four years without the loyal enthusiasm of its women and their loving ministrations.

Under the inspiration and energy of these Confederate women, homes again became homes, fields blossomed, order and system at last reigned after those terrible Reconstruction days.

The words of our beloved chieftain, Robert E. Lee, tell how our Southland rose, rebuilt by determined and courageous men and women of the Confederacy.

"We went home but our work was not completed, and it looked for awhile like the fortunate part of the Confederate army had 'crossed the river,' but with the same grit in peace that our boys had shown in war, they did not sit down and whine but went to work and thank God, through the spirit of their splendid example, our beloved Southland is more and more coming into her own as the days go by, and is already the choice part of the great and glorious Union."

"For out of the gloom
Future brightness is born;
As after the night
Looms the sunrise of morn."

In the face of overwhelming duties these noble women began the custom of annually decorating the graves of their soldier dead, thus bringing into existence the Southern Memorial Association. They commemorated the valor of the Confederate soldier in memorials through many a self-denial, as money was very scarce. They struggled for a home and pensions for the disabled soldiers and organized themselves and their descendents into a body of women, the United Daughters of the Confederacy, to preserve the history of their Confederacy. No, what the North Carolina women of the Sixties have done can never be forgotten by a State that loves to honor loyalty and self sacrifice.

Most of these heroic women have passed into the Beyond, but may their memories remain with us. They were modest, unassuming women, with no thought of what the world or coming generations would place upon the deeds of heroism and self-sacrifice.

"To us they live, an inspiration and a glory;
The flight of years can bring no rust,
To dim their fame in song and story."

It was left to that knightly soldier, Col. Ashley Horne of Clayton, to erect, in 1914, the only monument in North Carolina to the women of the Confederacy. This beautiful memorial stands in the Capitol grounds at Raleigh as a faithful witness to the sacrifice, heroism, and loyalty of our women of the Sixties. This "hero in times of war and patriot in times of peace," in giving this monument to the State, said: "The silent woman of the Memorial will typify the uncomplaining woman of the Confederacy."

In accepting this memorial for the State, Gov. Locke Craig said, "This statue is epic. Its theme is heroism and devotion; the inheritance of the children of the South. The bronze group represents the grandmother, unrolling [to] the eager youth, grasping the sword of his father, the scroll of the father's deeds. The statue is illumined with unfolding meaning.

"Women of the Confederacy, 'Henceforth all generations shall call you blessed.'"

The following just tribute was paid the women of the Confederacy of North Carolina and is preserved among the State Laws of 1862–63. "This General Assembly hereby records its heartfelt gratitude to the noble women of this State, who have done so much to alleviate the suffering of our soldiers and to sustain our righteous cause, and the Governor may, if he thinks expedient, record the distinguished names on the State's Roll of Honor."

On December 9, 1863, in a Resolution by the General Assembly, the following is incorporated:

"Equal to our appreciation of the valor and patriotism of our troops in the field is our admiration of the self-sacrificing and noble devotion of the women of our country in encouraging the soldiers on the way to the field of duty and of danger; in their untiring efforts to supply them with every comfort which their ingenuity can invent, and their indefatigable ministrations at the couch of the suffering, whether it be by disease or by wounds received in the defense of their country. This devotion to the cause of independence for which we are struggling is alike sustaining to the soldier on duty and the patriot at home and inspire[s] all with that energy which enables us to work with confidence to its successful termination and in a Confederate Government established upon an equitable basis and entitled to the highest possible position among the nations of the earth."

The record of North Carolina's women of the Sixties can only be compared with that of her "men in gray."

In her devotion to her country, in duty and bravery and all that goes to make up a splendid woman, the world has no superior example than the Woman of the Confederacy.

> "Who bade us go, with smiling tears?
> Who scorned the renegade?
> Who, silencing their trembling fears,
> Watched, cheered, then wept and prayed?
>
> "Who nursed their wounds with tender care,
> [And then, when all was lost,]
> Who lifted us from our despair
> And counted not the cost?
> The women of the South."

NORTH CAROLINA VERSES OF THE SIXTIES

"Poets are all who love,—who feel great truths, and tell them."

Answer to The Conquered Banner

(By Miss Sarah Ann Tillinghast, Fayetteville, N.C., written in 1865)

"Touch it not—unfold it never, Let it droop there, furled forever, For its people's hopes are dead!" (Father Ryan's "The Conquered Banner")

> *No, fold it not away forever,*
> *Keep it in hearts' depth ever,*
> *Love it, keep it for its past;*
> *Take it out some time and wave it,*
> *Think of those who died to save it,*
> *Glory in the blood we gave it,*
> *Bind it with our heart-strings fast.*
>
> *Take it out sometime and show it,*
> *Let your children early know it,*
> *Know its glory—not its shame.*
> *Teach them early to adore it,*
> *Scorn forever those who tore it,*
> *Tell them how it won a name.*
> [.....]

'Tis a witness how secession
Threw the glove down to oppression
Scorning at the last, concession,
Giving life blood for the right.
Oh, we cannot, cannot lose it,
(Oh how could the world refuse it?)
Can we let the foe abuse it
Or its history bright?
[. . . . .]
In future years some hand may take it
From its resting place and shake it
O'er the young and brave,
And the old spirit still undaunted
In their young hearts by God implanted
Will triumph o'er foes who vaunted
And freedom to the South be granted,
Though now there's none to save.

Though folded now away so sadly
In future years we'll wave it gladly,
In prosperous path we'll tread.
And thousands yet un-born shall hail it,
Tens of thousands never fail it,
Forgotten be the men who wail it—
Hated those who now can trail it—
Oh, can our hopes be dead?

Reconstruction

(By Mrs. Fannie Downing, written in the Sixties)

To die for Dixie! Oh, how blest
Are those who early went to rest,
Nor knew the future's awful store,
But deemed the cause the fought for sure
As heaven itself; and so laid down
The cross of earth for glory's crown,
    And nobly died for Dixie.

To live for Dixie! Harder put!
To stay the hand, to still the heart,
To seal the lips, enshroud the past,
To have no future—all o'ercast;
To knit life's broken threads again,
And keep her mem'ry pure from strain,
    This is to live for Dixie.

Carolina's Dead

By Miss Sarah Ann Tillinghast
(Written for the unveiling of the Cumberland County Confederate Monument, May 10th, 1902)

Uncoffined on the battle-field,
Those dreamless ones are sleeping,
Unconscious of the memories
Left in hearts that still are weeping—
Weeping for those that never came—
Brothers, and friends, and lovers,
Those gallant ones whose precious forms
    Virginia's soil now covers.
[. . . . .]
Then raise your monumental stone
To tell the grand old story
How splendidly her soldier boys
Fought for the old State's glory!
And let the little children know
The flag their fathers died for,
Teach them the cause they loved in vain.
    The principles they tried for.

For is not true, tried patriot love
A corner-stone worth trying,
O'er which to build our country up?
Then not in vain their dying.
And when this day comes yearly round
Get out the flag, and wave it
Above the record of their deeds
    Of those who died to save it.

The Woman of the Confederacy

(Written by poet Henry Jerome Stockard for unveiling of
the Confederate Woman's Monument in 1914)

She calmly brought his sabre bright,
  Tempered with death;
And, girding him, her all, aright,
And spoke with eyes of kindling light
  More than tongue uttereth.

And then she waved farewell at last,
  With grief struck dumb,
As bannered squadrons hurried past,
And bugles with imperious blast
  Stammered delirium.

The canvas can not hold her grace;
  Its colors warm
The damps of centuries erase;
Yet o'er the scathing years her face
Will live beyond all harm.

Not yet may story guard the trust,
  Nor song divine;
They, like their builders, turn to dust:—
Beyond corrupting moth and rust
  Stands, veiled with light, her shrine.

And Love will keep it, Love alone,
  Safe from decay,—

Love wherewith God himself is one—
When time's role shall be overthrown,
And earth shall pass away.

Nor bronze nor stone shall bear her name
Through time to-be:
These may be touched by frost or flame
And sink on ruin, while her fame
Is for eternity.

[**Note:** These are but a few of the "Stanzas" composed and read by Stockard at the 1914 unveiling of the memorial to the North Carolina Women of the Confederacy in Raleigh. The updated text presented here varies slightly from Mrs. Anderson's 1926 transcription. The full text may be found in the archives of East Carolina University and is reproduced at www.lib.ecu.edu/ncc/historyfiction/document/noa/entire.html.]

Gloria Victis

By Mrs. Francis P. Tiernan ("Christian Reid"). Written at the unveiling of the monument at Salisbury in memory of the Confederate dead, representing the group of a dying Confederate soldier supported and crowned by fame.

No warrior of the golden past, of glorious antique days,
Crowned with the victor wreath of Greece, or Rome's immortal bays,
No knight who laid his lance in rest with mighty Charlemagne,
Or bore the brave crusader's cross in great St. Louis' train.

But the heir of all these heroes of the great days of old,
Last of the long and gallant line of knightly hearts of gold,
One who has written with his sword his name upon the page
Of glory's deathless muster-roll, gathered from every age.

A soldier of the Southern Cross, a hero of the cause
Of the sacred right of Sovereign States, of chartered claims and laws
Which sprang from the great Charter, wrung by the barons bold
From a craven king of Runnymede, in the brave times of old.

In bronze he is before us here, this patriot of our land;
This type of all the gallant men who ever more shall stand
For all of human valor, for all of noble worth,
And for all of dauntless courage that has glorified the earth.

A stripling, so we see him, one of the great array
Of the young South who sprang to arms without an hour's delay,

Leaving the sports of boyhood, leaving the work of men,
Turning away from the sunny life, they never could know again.

Up with a smile in the saddle, to ride and fight and fly,
Or marshaled into serried ranks to stand and fight and die,
Storming with reckless daring the heights of shot and shell,
Or dashing with reckless might into the jaws of hell.

Who does not know the story? See, you can read it there,
Told in its matchless glory, told in its last despair.
Look! He has fought to the utmost, stripped for the last hard fight,
Fought till his gun is broken, and the bitter end is in sight.

Then, as he falls exhausted, with face of noble calm.
The steadfast face of a hero, worthy a martyr's palm,
Then as he sinks in dying, lo! from that realm afar,
Where justice holds her even scale above the chance of war.

A splendid form has swept the earth, to bear him in her clasp,
'Tis Glory, with the laurel-wreath of fame within her grasp!
And on the vanquished hero's brow her hand will place that wreath,
The symbol of immortal fame beyond the reach of death.

INDEX

1st N.C. Regiment, 78; Co. A, 82–83
1st N.C. Cavalry, 117, 141
6th Infantry State Troops, 135
6th N.C. Regiment, 38, 101; Co. I (Forsyth County), 138–39 141
11th N.C. Regiment, Co. C, 137
20th N.C. Regiment, Co. E, 140
26th N.C. Regiment, 12–13

Aid Society (of Chatham County), 73
aid society of Wadesboro, 39
Alamance County, N.C., 153, 156, 160, 163, 164
Albemarle (Confederate ironclad), 84–85
Alford, G. H., 151–52
Alford, George Benton, 151–52
Alford, Mrs. Rebecca Jones (wife of G. H. Alford), 151–52
Allen, Andrew, 162
Allen, Mrs. Hamlin, home of, 78
Allen, James, 162
Allen, Mrs. Rebecca Moore (wife of James J. Allen), 162
Allen, Thomas, 162
Allen, William, 162
Allston, Philip, 160
Allston, Mrs. Samuel T., 160
Alston, Miss Maria, 144
Anderson, Mrs. (of Fayetteville, N.C.), 29
Anderson, Lucy Worth London (Mrs. John Huske Anderson), v
Anderson, Miss Maggie, 146
Andrews, Allen, 163
Andrews, Mrs. Delany, 163
Andrews, Hezekiah, 163
Andrews, Thomas, 163
Anson County, N.C., 39, 60–62, 161
Anson Guards, 135
Ansonville, N.C., 134
"Answer to the Conquered Banner" (poem), 72, 103
Archbell, Mrs. Lillie, 57

Arrington Mrs. Kathrine (daughter of V. L. Pendelton), 104
Ashe family (of Rocky Point, N.C.), 126–27
Ashe, Maj. John Grange, 126
Ashe, Mary Porter, 126–27
Ashe, Capt. Samuel A., 29, 50–51, 62, 105–6, 126–27
Ashe, Hon. William S., 126
Asheboro, N.C., 115, 136, 163
Asheville, N.C., 86–88
Askew, Edward, 160
Askew, Levi, 160
Askew, Richard, 160
Askew, Wilbur, 160
Askew, Zephaniah, 160
Askew, Mrs. Zephaniah (Lucretia), 160
Atkinson, Bishop Thomas, 62
Atkinson, Bishop, wife of, 39
Attmore, Hannah (Mrs. Dolph J. Long), 18
Attmore, Miss Mary, 17–18
Attmore, Thomas, 18
"Aunt Abby, the Irrepressible" (Mary Bayard Clarke), 58–60
"Aunt Amelia," of Holt family, Lexington, 123
Aunt Harriet, servant of Miller family, 75
Averasboro, N.C., 54, 149–50, 155
Avery, Maj., 159
Avery, Mrs. Isaac, 159

Bailey, Judge Lancaster, 86–88
Bailey, Sarah Jane (Mrs. William Cain), 86–87
Bailey, Thomas, 87–88
Baker, Mrs. Flora, 162
Barham, Ensign W. K., 134
Barnes, Mrs. Edna, 161
Barrett, Mary Ann Tilden, v
Barringer, Gen. Paul, 159, 163
Bason, Mrs. Celia D., 163
Bason, George, 163

Bason, James, 163
Bason, William, 163
Battle, Mrs. Frederick (Tempie Perry), 162
Battle, Dr. Kemp, 100
Battle, Tempie Ann (Mrs. Marriott), 116–17
Beaman, Mrs. (superintendent of the North Carolina Confederate Woman's Home) *see* Murphy, Mary Bailey
Beasley, Mrs. (of Plymouth, N.C.), 12
Beaufort, N.C., 16, 36
Beauregard, Gen. P. G. T., 37, 69
Beckwith, Mrs. Evelyn Smith, 64
Bedham, Capt. William, 83
Beeman, Mrs. Lem, 135
Belo Home (Forsyth County), 139
Belo, Capt. A. H., 138–39
Belo, Miss Nellie, 138–39
Bennett, Miss Charlotte, 62
Bennett, Frank, 161
Bennett, Mrs. Jane, 61–62
Bennett, John, 161
Bennett, L. D., family of, 61–62; home of, 61–62
Bennett, Miss Mary, 61–62
Bennett, Capt. Risden Tyler, 135
Bennett, Mrs. Risden Tyler (Kate Shepherd), 39
Bennett, Mrs. Samuel (Jane Little), 161
Bennett, Thomas, 161
Bennett, William, 161
Bentonville, N.C., 35, 53, 68, 155
Bertie County, N.C., 78, 137
Best, B. J., 158
Best, Henry, 158
Best, Mrs. Henry (Maria Edmundson), 158
Best, R. E., 158
Best, Robert, 158
Best, T. H., 158
Best, William E., 158
Bethel Regiment, 38, 140–41
Bethune, Mrs. Lauchlan, 162
Betsy, in Holt household, 122
Beverly, Miss Fan, 39
Biographical History of North Carolina (Ashe), 29
Black family (of Buncombe County), 155, 156
Bladen County, N.C., 93, 156

Blalock, Mr. (of Caldwell County, N.C.), 12
Blalock, Mrs. L. M., (of Caldwell County, N.C.), 12
Bland Wood (home of Mrs. Morehead, Guilford County), 69
Blount, Gen. W. A., 36
Blount, Mr. George W., 79
Blount, Miss Patsy B., aunt of, 36
Blythe, Mrs., of Philadelphia, 139
Bombshell (Confederate tender), 84
Bowden, Mrs. Able, 157
Branch, Gen., 52, 147–48
Branch, Mrs. L. O'B. (widow of Gen. Branch), 148
Brem's Battery (Charlotte), 112
Brockman, Mrs. Thomas M., 119
Brooks, Mrs. Blacknall (Bettie Lemly), 138–39
Brown (U.S.) Gen., 88
Brown, Miss Camelia, 91
Browning, Maj. John, farm of, 117
Brownlaw, Miss (of Warren County), 144
Brunswick County, N.C., 78–79
Buncombe County, N.C., 86–89, 155
Buncombe Riflemen, 136
Burke County, N.C., 90, 156, 159
Burnside, (U.S.) Gen., 69, 81
Burton, Capt. A. W., 138
Burwell, Armistead, 158
Burwell, Dandridge Spottswood, 158
Burwell, James Webb, 158
Burwell, John Bott, 158
Burwell, Robert Turnbull, 158
Burwell, Mrs. Robert (Margaret Robertson), 38, 157
Burwell, William Robertson, 158
Buxton Place (home of Mrs. John Buxton Williams, Warren County), 161
Byrd, Lt. Col. Francis W., 137

Cabarrus County, N.C., 160
Cain, Mrs. William (Sarah Jane Bailey), 86–87
Caldwell County, N.C., 12–13
Caldwell, Mrs. J. P., 143
Caldwell County, N.C., 90
Calvary Church, Tarboro, 112
Camcill, Mrs. James, 92
Cameron, Col. Benehan, 31, 129

Cameron, Donald Moore, 33
Cameron, Paul, 32
Cameron, Mrs. Paul, 32
Cameron, Miss Rebecca, 32
Cameron, Mrs. William, 32
Campbell, Miss Alice, 23–24, 124, 146
Campbell, Miss Mary, 124, 146
Cape Fear Chapter, Daughters of the Confederacy, 120
Cape Fear Chapter #3, U.D.C., v, vii
Cape Henry, Va., 80
Carlton, Mrs. Thomas, 159
Carlton, Mrs. Thomas, son-in-law of (William), 159
Carolina and the Southern Cross (magazine), 57
"Carolina's Dead" (poem), 103, 174
Carson, Col. Logan, home of (Marion, McDowell County), 89–90
Carson, Mrs. J. H., 37
Carteret County, N.C., 14
Caswell County, N.C., 140
Cedar Fork community, Wake County, N.C., 140–42
Cedar Vale (home near Elizabeth City), 80
Ceres (Federal gunboat), 84
Chadwick, Mrs. Polly, 94
Chaffee, Daisy (wife of Col. William Lamb), 66–67
Chamberlain, Mrs. Hope Summerell, 98–99
Chance, Andrew Jackson, 162
Chance, Mrs. Sarah Williams (wife of Tillman F. Chance), 162
Chance, Tillman Franklin, Jr., 162
Chance, William Anderson, 162
Chandler, Mrs. Thomas, 158
Chapel Hill, N.C., 99–100
Charlotte Female Institute, 38, 105
Charlotte Grays, 142–43
Charlotte Grays, 38
Charlotte Journal (newspaper), 105
Charlotte navy yard, 112
Charlotte, N.C., 36–39, 142–43, 158; churches, 112
"Chase, The" (poem), 41
Chatham County, N.C., 73, 154, 161
Chicora Cemetery (Smithville), 53–54
Chicora Chapter, Daughters of the Confederacy, 151

Children's Chapter, Daughters of the Confederacy, 125
Childs, Col. Frederick, home of, 29
Childs, Col. Frederick, mother of, 29–30
Childs, Jennie (sister of Col. Frederick Childs), 29
Chowan River, 83
Christ Church (Raleigh), 51–52
"Christian Reid" (pseud. of Frances Fisher Tiernan), 100–102, 177–78
"Church Bells of the Confederacy, The" (poem), 113
Clark, Mrs. Boone, 90
Clark's *N.C. Histories*, 19
Clarke, Col. William J., 102
Clarke, Mrs. Mary Bayard (wife of Col. William J. Clarke), 58–60, 102–3
Clayton, N.C., 168
Clinton, N.C., 63–63
Cole, J. C., 15
Cole, J. L., 15
Cole, Mrs. M. C., 16
Coleraine, Bertie County, N.C., 78
Collection of Letters and Papers of President Davis, 118
Com. Hull (Federal gunboat), 84
Commissary Department (Granville), 124
Company A, 1st Regiment N.C. State Troops, 82–83
Company C, 11th N.C. Regiment, 137
Company E, 20th N.C. Regiment, 140
Company I (Forsyth County), 138–39
Company I, 6th N.C. Regiment, 141
Condor (blockade runner), 44
Confederate Bible Society, 129
Confederate Hospital (Charlotte), 37
Confederate Treasury Department, 125
Cook, Capt. (commander of the *Albemarle*), 84–85
Corbett, Mrs. Mary A. (mother of Mary Bailey Murphy), 19–20, 63–64
Corbett, Mrs. Mary A., infant child of, 63–64
Cotton Plant (Confederate tender), 84
Cowan, Mrs. Robert H., 28
Cox, Gen., 52
Craig, Gov. Locke, 168
Craten, Capt. M. D., 140
Craven County, N.C., 64

Creecy, Col. Richard, 79–80
Crenshaw, Miss Cornelia, 137
Croaker, Mrs. (of Kinston), 94
Cromwell, Col. Elisha, 116
Cromwell, Mrs. Margaret Ann (wife of Col. Elisha Cromwell), 116
Cross Creek, Fayetteville, N.C., viii, 49, 145–46
Crutchfield, Mrs. M. L. (Margaret Holt), 69–70
Cumberland County Militia, 21
Cumberland County War Association, Fayetteville, 24
Cumberland County, N.C., 21–25, 94–96, 109, 154, 155–56
Curtis, John Henry, 111
Curtis, Mrs. M. A., 111

Davidson, John, 162
Davidson, Mrs. Mary (Laura King), 162
Davidson, Richard, 162
Davidson, Robert, 162
Davis, Mrs. B. C., 148–49
Davis, Mrs. D. A., 91
Davis, Mrs. Junius, 28
Davis, Pres. Jefferson, 38, 59–60, 117–18
Davis, Pres. Jefferson and Mrs., 69
Davis Mrs. Jefferson, and children, 128
Davis, Maggie (daughter of Jefferson Davis), 118
De Mille, Miss Margaret, 35
Deanes, Mrs. Harriett, 164
Deanes, James, 164
Deanes, Jefferson, 164
Deanes, John, 164
Deaton, Aaron, 155
Deaton, Caleb, 154
Deaton, Cornelius, 155
Deaton, Edward, 155
Deaton, George, 155
Deaton, Mrs. James (Sarah Goodman), 154
Deaton, John, 155
Deaton, Pinckney, 155
Deaton, Samuel, 155
Deaton, Thomas, 155
Maj. De Meille, Maj. (brother-in-law of Miss E. M. B. Hoyt), 124
Denem, Capt., *see* Denson, Capt. C. B.
Denson, Capt. C. B., 140

DeRosset, Armand, 157
DeRosset, Mrs. Armand J. (Eliza Lord), 26–27, 146–47, 157
DeRosset, Mrs. Armand, sons-in-law of, 157
DeRosset, Catherine (Mrs. William Kennedy), 12
DeRosset, Edward, 157
DeRosset, Gabrielle (Mrs. A. M. Waddell), 41–43
DeRosset, John, 157
DeRosset, Louis, 157
DeRosset, Mrs. Louis, 28
DeRosset, Mrs. Louis H., 41–43
DeRosset, Thomas, 157
DeRosset, William, 157
Devereux, Miss Anne, 148
Devereux, Mrs. John, 148
Devereux, Thomas Polk, 102
Dixon, Mrs. Alex, 158
Dockery, Mrs. Henry, 149
Downing, Mrs. Fannie, 103–4, 173
Dunn Chapter, U.D.C., 149
Dunn, N.C., 151
Duplin County, N.C., 71–72, 140
Durham, Miss Julia (Mrs. Green), 138

Edenton, N.C., and Albemarle region, 81–85; churches, 112
Edgecombe County, N.C., 117
Edgecombe Guards, 137
Edgeworth Seminary (Greensboro), 68
Edwards, Mrs. Jesse, 39
Elizabeth City, N.C., 52, 79–81
Elliott, Gilbert, 85
Elliott, Mrs. (of Elizabeth City), 80
Elliott, Mrs. Sarah E., 52–53
Ellis, Gov., 128, 135
Ellis, Mrs. A. J., 141–42
Ellison, Miss (of Fayetteville), 124
Ellison, Miss Annie, 78
Elmwood Cemetery (Charlotte), 37
Enfield Blues, 78

Faison, N.C., 71–72
Fayetteville Independent Light Infantry, 23, 141
Fayetteville, "an old lady of," 94–95
Fayetteville, N.C., viii, 21–25, 29, 45–47, 94–95, 124, 140–41, 145–46, 161,

163; arsenal, 124, 127; churches; 111; hospital, 45–49; Marine Hospital, Fayetteville, 46–47
Fearing, Capt., 80–81
Fearing, Mrs. Molly E. (wife of Capt. Fearing), 80–81
Federal cemetery (Raleigh), 54
Female Academy (Salem), 74
Finch, Mrs. Henry, 64
First Bethel Regiment, 143
Fisher, Col., 135
Fisher, Col. Charles F., 101
Fisher, Miss Christine, 135
Fore, Mrs. J. A., 142
Forsyth County, N.C., 74, 138
Forsyth Rifles, 139
Fort Barstow, Roanoke Island, N.C., 80–81
Fort Fisher, 27, 42, 66–67
Fort Macon, 136, 140
Foster, (U.S.) Gen., 35
Foy, Franklin, scout, 65
Foy, Mrs. Rachael (widow of Enoch Foy), 65
Franklin County, N.C., 39–40, 58–60, 157, 158, 160, 162
Franklin Rifles, 134
French Mrs. George (Nellie Worth), 65
Fries, Miss Carrie, 138–39
Fries, Mary (Mrs. Rufus Lenoir Patterson), 138–39
Fuquay Springs, N.C., 31

Gaines, Miss (of Asheville), 136
Gainey, Mrs. A. McA., 109
Garman, Mrs. Thomas, 158
Garrett, Mrs. (of Ansonville), 134–35
Gatlin, (U.S.) Gen., 34
"General Lee at the Battle of the Wilderness" (poem), 102
Gibbs, Mrs. Margaret Smith, 162
Gibbs, Robert, 162
Gibbs, Thomas, 162
Gibbs, William, 162
Gill, Benjamin, 160
Gill, Frank, 160
Gill, Miss Isabell, 125
Gill, James, 160
Gill, John, 160
Gill, Mrs. Sarah Jones, 160

Gill, Thomas, 160
Gillam, (U.S.) Gen., 87
Gillette, Mrs. (of New Bern), 65–66
"Gloria Victis" (poem), 102, 177–78
Goldsboro Rifles, 140
Goldsboro, N.C., 34–35
Graham place (near Kinston), 75
Graham, Gov. William, 32
Graham, Mrs. W. A. (William A.), 32, 33
Granville County, N.C., 154, 157, 158
Green, Capt. W. F., 134
Green, Col. (of Warren County), 144–45
Green, Julia (Durham), 138
Green, Mrs. Wharton (wife of Col. Green), 144–45
Greenhow, Mrs. Rose O'Neal, 43–44, 67
Greenhow, Mrs. Rose O'Neal, daughter of, 44
Greensboro, N.C., 33, 59–60, 68–69; boarding school, 105; churches, 112
Grier, Laban, 163
Grier, Mrs. Andrew (Margaret Barringer, daughter of Gen. Paul Barringer), 163
Grier, Mrs. Andrew (Margaret Barringer), stepson of (Thomas), 163
Grier, Samuel, 163
Grier, William, 163
Guilford County, N.C., 69, 157
Guion hotel (Raleigh), 50
Guion, Mrs. (of Fayetteville), 49

Halifax County, N.C., 141, 156; 163
Halifax, N.C., churches, 112
Hall of History (Raleigh), 129 134, 135, 136, 140, 141, 142
Hammond, Mrs. Hampton B., 135
Hampton, Gen. Wade, 47
Hargrove, Mrs. Sallie Lancaster, 160
Harnett County, N.C., 155
Harper, Mrs. (of Lenoir), 90
Harper, Mrs. John, 53
Hart, Abigail (Mrs. Julius Lewis), 17
Hatteras, N.C., 80
Haw River, N.C., 69
Haywood, Mrs. Martha, 51–52
Heath, Mrs. Mary Morrow, 158
Heck, Miss (of Warren County), 144
Heinzerling, Mrs. J. E. (daughter of Tillman Franklin Chance, Jr.), 162

Henderson, Dr. Archibald, 86–87
Henry, Dellia Maria (Mrs. Anderson Roscoe Miller), 74–77
Hertford County, N.C., 160, 163, 164
Hicks, Albert, 72
Hicks, Dr. James H., 71, 72
Hicks, Dr. John, 72
Hicks, Elias, 72
Hicks, Mrs. Eliza (Mrs. James H. Hicks), 71, 72
Hicks, John, 72
Hicks, Capt. Lewis, 72
Hicks, Lewis T., 140
Hicks, Lt. A. D., 72
Hicks, Lyde, 72
Hicks, Miss Georgia, 71, 72, 110
High Point, N.C., 92
Hill, Mrs. C. D., 71–72
Hill, Col. (Gen.) D. H., 38, 103, 143, 159
Hill, Col., of Faison, servants of, 110
Hill, Cynthia, servant of Hill family, 110
Hill, Eliza (Mrs. William Lord), 28
Hillsborough, N.C., 31–34; 130; churches, 33, 111
Hines, Dr. Peter, 12
Holt family and household, Lexington, 120–23
Holt, Amelia (daughter of Mrs. William R. Holt), 120–23
Holt, Claudia (daughter of Mrs. William R. Holt), 120–23
Holt, Frances (daughter of Mrs. William R. Holt), 120–23
Holt, Francis (Mrs. C. A. Hunt), 120
Holt, Louisa Hogan, wife of (Dr. William R. Holt), 121, 120–23, 161
Holt, Margaret (Mrs. M. L. Crutchfield), 69–70
Holt, Tempie Whitehead, 117
Holt, Dr. William R., 121–23
Holt, Mrs. William R. (Louisa Hogan), 121, 120–23, 161
Holton, E. J., 105
Holton, Rachael (Mrs. E. J.), 105
Homestead, the, home of Holt family, Lexington, 120–23
Hope Mills, N.C., 47
Horne, Col. Ashley, 168
Horne, Mrs. Ashley, 161

Hornet's Nest Rifles (Charlotte), 38, 78, 142–43
House, Mrs. Abby Horne, 58–60
Howard, (U.S.) Gen., 72
Howell, Miss Hattie, 143
Howland, Mrs. Elizabeth Carraway, 16
Howley, (U.S.) Gen., 87–88
Hoy, Miss M. M., 35, 36
Hoyt, Miss Clara, 136–37
Hoyt, Miss E. M. B., 124
Hunt, Miss Camille Holt, 120–23
Huske, Rev. Dr. Joseph C., 49, 145–46
Hyatt, Mrs. H. O., 74–75

Ingle, Albert, 160
Ingle, Mrs. David, 160
Ingle, Mabin, 160
Ingle, Rufus, 160
Ingle, Sidney, 160
Ingle, Thaddeus, 160
Iredell County, N.C., 92, 154, 159
Iredell, Miss Margaret, 148
Ivanhoe community, Sampson County, N.C., 63–64

Jackson, Mrs. Anna Morrison, 114–15
Jackson, Mrs. John (Lucy Worth), 73
Jackson, Stonewall, 159
James, Mrs. Josh T. (Mary London), 73
Jerry, butler of Holt family, Lexington, 121
Johnson, Miss Anna, 125
Johnston County, 64, 157, 161
Johnston, Dr. Charles, 50
Johnston, Gen. Joseph E., 53, 55, 69
Johnston, Mrs. Sloan, 91
Jones, Alexander (Sandy), 154
Jones, Archibald, 154
Jones, Mrs. Armistead, 147–48
Jones, Daniel, 154
Jones, Dougal, 154
Jones, Duncan, 154
Jones, Eliza Ann, 31
Jones, Hiram, 154
Jones, James, 154
Jones, John, 154
Jones, Mrs. Joseph, 145
Jones, Mrs. Joseph Speed, 144
Jones, Mrs. Lucinda, 144
Jones, Malcolm, 154

Jones, Mrs. Reuben (Flora Macdonald), 153
Jones, Samuel, 154
Jones, William, 154
Jones's Sulphur Springs, 144
Joyner, Edmund, 164
Joyner, John, 164
Joyner, Mrs. William (Emily), 160, 164
Joyner, Robert, 164
Juvenile Knitting Society, Fayetteville, 25

Kas, coachman in Holt household, Lexington, 123
Kennedy, Mrs. William (Catherine DeRosset), 12
Kennedy, Mrs. William (Rose Roundtree), 66
Kilpatrick, (U.S.) Gen., 69, 121–23
Kinston, N.C., 34, 57–58, 66, 74–77, 94; U.D.C. in, 74
Kirk (U.S.) Gen., 86, 92
Kittrell Springs, N.C., hospital, 52¬–53
Kittrell, N.C., 52–53
Kyle, Mrs. Jesse (Anne K.), 45, 145–46

Ladies Aid Society (of Hillsborough), 32
Ladies Memorial Association (of Charlotte), 37
Ladies Memorial Association of Wilmington, 146–47
Ladies Memorial Association, Wake County, 147–48
Ladies Memorial Association, Wilmington, 44
"Lady Dela Crucis, The" (poem), 101–2
LaFayette Company, 141
LaFayette Light Infantry, 24
Lamb, Col. William, 66
Lamb, Mrs. William (Daisy Chaffee), 66–67
Land of the Sky, The (Tiernan, 1874), 101
Land We Love, The (magazine), 103
Last Ninety Days of the War in North-Carolina, The (Spencer), 90, 98, 100
Last Words of Confederate Heroes (Pendleton), 104–5
Laurinburg, N.C., 28, 134, 157
Lee, Gen. Robert E., 69
Lee, Gen. Robert E., brother of, 69
Lee, Miss Anne Carter, 144

Leeds, Miss Anne Mason, 148
"Leigh, Stuart" (pseud. of Mary Bayard Clarke), 103
Lemly, Bettie (Mrs. Blacknall Brooks), 138–39
Lemly, Miss Laura, 138–39
Lenoir, N.C., 89–90, 92, 161
Lewis, Mrs. Julius (Abigail Hart), 17
Lexington, N.C., 120–23, 159, 161
Light Infantry, Fayetteville, 78
Light Infantry, Halifax, 78
Light Infantry, Wilmington, 78
Light Infantry, Wilson, 78
Lincoln County, N.C., 158
Linwood, plantation owned by Holt family, Lexington, 121–23
Little River community (Harnett and Cumberland Counties, N.C.)
Little, Mrs. Eugene, 135
London, Henry Armand, 163
London, Mrs. Henry A. (Bettie Worth), 73
London, Mrs. Henry A. (Sallie Lord), 163
London, Mrs. Henry Armand, 110–13
London, Miss Mary (Mrs. Josh T. James), 73
London, Rufus Marsden, 163
London, William Lord, 163
Long, Jacob, 164
Long, Mrs. J. Dolph (Hannah Attmore), 18
Long, Mrs. Lettie Jones, 164
Long, Robert, 164
Long, Thomas, 164
Longstreet community, Cumberland County, N.C., 155–56
Longstreet's battle, 47
Lord, Eliza (Mrs. Armand J. DeRosset), 26–27
Lord, Mrs. William (Eliza Hill), 28
Louisburg, N.C., 39–40, 133–34
Lowe, Mrs. (Fannie Lyon), 142
Lynx (blockade runner), 41–42
Lyon, Miss Fannie (Mrs Lowe), 142
Lyon, Miss Jennie, 142

Mallett, Miss Carrie, 145–46
Mallett, Miss Maggie, 145–46
Malone, Mr. J. E., 134
Mammy Caroline, servant in childhood home of Mrs. F. C. Roberts, 108

Mandy, maid in Holt household, Lexington, 123
Manly, Miss (of Washington), 136
Manly, Mrs. Charles (wife of Gov. Manly), 163
Manly, Mrs. Charles (wife of Gov. Manly), sons and sons-in-law of, 163
Manly's Battery, Raleigh, 127–28
Maria, in Holt household, 122
Marion, N.C., 89–90
Marorie, Miss Martha, 136
Marriott, Dr. (husband of Tempie Ann Battle Marriott), 117
Marriott, Mrs. Tempie Ann (Battle), 116–17
Marshall, Capt. James K., 82
Martin, Gen. James G., 87
Martin, Mrs. (of Elizabeth City). 80
Martin, Mrs. Alfred, 26
Masonic Home (Greensboro), 69
Mattabessett (Federal gunboat), 84
McCallum, Mrs. Jessie, 91
McCatten, Mrs. Angus, 161
McCorkle, Capt. M. L., 159
McDanial, Mrs. Funifold (Kate Harrison), 161
McDaniel, Mrs. John, 30
McDaniel, Mrs. Thomas, 31
McDowell County, N.C., 89–90
McGougan, Alexander, 162
McGougan, Daniel, 162
McGougan, Mrs. Duncan (Annie White), 162
McGougan, James, 162
McGougan, Reuben, 162
McGuffey Readers, 130
McIver, Miss Rachael, 72–73, 140
McKethan, Augustus, 163
McKethan, Edward, 163
McKethan, Mrs. Edward, 163
McKethan, Hector, 163
McKimmon, Miss Kate, 127–29
McLaurin, Miss Kate, 146
McLean, Mrs. Neal, 157
McNair, Mrs. Anna, 137
McNeill, Mr. (of Cumberland County) and family, 96–97
McRae, James, 161
McRae, John, 161

McRae, Mrs. John (Mary Shackleford), 161
McRae, Mrs. John (Mary Shackleford), stepson of (Duncan), 161
McRae, Robert, 161
McRae, Thomas, 161
Mecklenburg County, N.C., 36–39, 104, 162, 163
Meekins, Mrs. A. M., 17
"Melt the Bells" (poem), 83
Memorial Association (Fayetteville), 145–46
Memorial Association (New Bern), 148–49
Memorial Association (of Raleigh), 50
Memorial Association (Tarboro), 49
"Memorial Flowers" (poem), 103
Memorial Society, Averasboro, 149–50
Mercer, Mrs. John, 78–79
Methodist Church, Wilmington, 27
Metts, Mrs. James I., 28
Miami (Federal gunboat), 84
Michels, Mrs. Sally, 156
Middleton, Mrs. Henry, 87
Military Institute (of Col. D. H. Hill, Charlotte), 38
Military Sewing Society, Washington, N.C., 35
Miller, Dr. [Anderson Roscoe], 74
Miller, Mrs. Anderson Roscoe (Dellia Maria Henry), 74–77
Miller, Dellia Maria, brother of (William), 77
Miller, Mrs. Henry, 148
Milton Blues, 140
Mitcherson, Mrs. Samuel, 158
Montgomery, Mrs. (of Rowan County), 91
Moore County, N.C., 160, 161, 162
Moore, Mrs., of Raleigh (daughter of the publisher, Mr. Branson), 105
Moore, Albert, 163
Moore, Evans, 156
Moore, Mrs. Godwin, 160
Moore, Harrison, 156
Moore, Haywood, 156
Moore, Isaac, 156
Moore, James, 160
Moore, Jefferson, 156
Moore, John, 160
Moore, Mrs. John, 163
Moore, John, 163

Moore, Julian, 160
Moore, Louis T., 67
Moore, Miss Mary E., 81–85
Moore, Solomon, 156
Moore, Thomas, 160
Moore, Mrs. Thomas (Rachael Jeffries), 156
Moore, William, 156, 160, 163
Mordecai, Mr. Henry, 148
Morehead City Chapter, U.D.C., 15
Morehead, Gov. James L., 68–69
Morehead, Mrs. James, 69
Morehead, Mrs. John, 37
Morgan, Mrs. Thomas, 157
Morganton, N.C., 92, 156, 159
Morris Island, S.C., 45
Morris, Miss (of Cedar Fork), 142
Morris, Alpheus, 164
Morris, Calvin, 164
Morris, Mrs. Carian, 164
Morris, William, 164
Morrison, Mrs. (of Davidson College; sister of Gov. Graham), 159
Morrison, Mrs. (of Davidson College), sons of, 159
Morrison, Mrs. Jackson Daniel Thrash, 116
Morrisville community, Wake County, N.C., 140–42
Morrisville Grays, 142
Morrisville, N.C., 32
Moseley, Mrs. Robert A., 63
Moseley, Mrs. Robert A., sisters of (including Anna and Ida), 63
Moseley, Robert A., home of, 63
Moseley, Robert, Jr. (infant son of Mr. and Mrs. Robert A. Mosely), 63
Murchison, Mr. (Cumberland County, N.C.), 30
Murchison, Mrs. Duncan, 30
Murphy, Mary Bailey (Mrs. Beaman), 19–20
Murphy, Miss Rebecca (Mrs. Benjamin Winborne), 132–34
Museum of the Confederacy (Richmond, Va.), 139; North Carolina room, 146
"Must I Forget" (poem), 102
Myers, Mrs. Thomas, 136–37

Nash County, N.C., 117, 158, 161, 162
Nelson house, in Rockfish section of Cumberland and Hoke Counties, 95
Nelson, Mrs. (of Rockfish), 95
New Bern, N.C., 14, 15–20, 65–66, 76, 94, 107–9, 125, 148–49, 159; battle, 112
Nichols, Maj. (Sherman's aide-de-camp), 29
Nichols, Mrs. Martha Thorne, 163
Niphon (Federal cruiser), 42
Nobles, Miss Ella, 134
N.C. Confederate Woman's Home, 20
N.C. Division, United Daughters of the Confederacy, v, 3, 18, 32, 71, 73, 78 101, 111, 115, 116, 117, 120, 133–34, 135, 141, 142, 162
N.C. Division, United Confederate Veterans, 60, 134, 164
N.C. General Assembly, 1863, 168–69
N.C. Hospital, Petersburg, Va., 12, 50
North Carolina Society, Colonial Dames, 43
North Carolina Whig (newspaper), 105
North, Miss Mary (daughter of Dr. Jonathan North), 94
Nutt, Eliza Hall (Mrs. William M. Parsley), 119–20

Oak Grove (home of John Smith), 53–54, 150
Oakdale Cemetery, Wilmington, 44, 147
Old Days in Chapel Hill (Spencer), 98
Olds, Col. F. A., 129
Onslow County, N.C., 158
Orange County, N.C., 158
Orange Light Artillery, 33
Osborne, Mrs. M. A., 37
"Our Division Song" (poem), 132
Outlaw, Capt. Edward, 137
Outlaw, Miss (of Bertie County), 137
Owen, Miss Fannie, 36
Owen, Mrs. Katherine Watkins, 33
Oxford, N.C., 52, 80

Padrick, Mrs. Hudlah, 158
Page, Lt. (of Cedar Fork), 142
Page, Miss (of Cedar Fork), 142
Palmer, Mrs. Oran Allston, 161
Parker, Miss Arabella Clark, 149
Parsley, Col. William M., 119
Parsley, Mrs. William M. (Eliza Hall Nutt), 119–20

Partridge, Miss Sophia, 148
Patterson, Mrs. Rufus Lenoir (Mary Fries), 138–39
Patton, Miss (of Asheville), 136
Patton Mrs. James W., 87, 88
Patton Mrs. James W., sister of, 88
Paxton, Mrs. (of Morganton), 92
Peace Institute (Raleigh), 50
Pearsal, Mrs. Rachel, 72
Pearsal, Mrs. Rachel, aunt of, 72
Pearson, Col. William, 156
Pendelton, Mrs. V. L. (Victoria Louise), 104–5
Pender County, N.C., 164–65
Pender, Capt. Josiah, 43
Pender, Mrs. Josiah (Laura), 43
Person, Mrs. Abia, 162
Pettigrew hospital (Raleigh), 50
Pettigrew, Miss M. L., 12, 50
Phifer, Mr. and Mrs. Wm. F., 37
Phillips, Frederick, 163
Phillips, Mrs. Harriet, 163
Phillips, James, 163
Phillips, Joseph, 163
Pigott, Miss Emmeline, 14, 16
Pitt County, N.C., 160, 163, 164
Pittsboro, N.C., 73, 111, 112, 154, 163
Pleasant Grove Baptist Church, Wake County, 151–52
Plymouth, N.C., 12, 84–85, 139; churches, 112
Poe, Miss Alice, 146
Polk, Gen. Leonidas, widow and daughter of, 92
Polk, Mrs. Lucy (Williams), 145
Pollock, Mr. Thomas, 112
Pool, Col. Stephen D., 18
Pridgen, Alexander, 161
Pridgen, Drewry, 161
Pridgen, Henry, 161
Pridgen, Josiah, 161
Pridgen, Mrs. Julia Anne, 164–65
Pridgen, M. B., 164–65
Pridgen, Mrs. William (Patsy Lindsay), 161
"Prison Mother, The," 16
Protestant Episcopal Church, Wilmington, 27
Pruden, Charles, 163
Pruden, Henry, 163

Pruden, John, 163
Pruden, Mrs. Lewis, 163

Raleigh Register (newspaper), 113
Raleigh, N.C., 12, 49–52; 102–3, 114, 127–29, 130, 148, 168; churches, 113; hospitals, 50
Ram (later the ironclad *Albermarle*), 84
Ramsay, Mrs. Margaret E., 91
Randolph County, N.C., 157
Rankin, Miss Emma L., 89–90
Ransom, Gen. Robert, 117–18, 141
Ransom, Mrs. Robert, 117–18
Ray, Polly, widow (of Longstreet community, Cumberland County), 155
"Rebel Sock" (poem) 102–3
"Reconstruction" (poem), 103, 173
Reed, Capt. *see* Reid, Capt.
"Regret" (poem), 102
Reid, Capt. (commander of the *Lynx*), 41–42
"Reid, Christian" (pseud. of Frances Fisher Tiernan), 100–102, 177–78
Richardson home, Anson County, N.C., 39
Ridgeway (School?), 117
Roanoke Island, N.C., 80
Robbins, Mrs. Alvi (Mary Brown), 157
Robbins, Franklin Childs, 157
Robbins, James LaFayette, 157
Robbins, Julius Alexander, 157
Robbins, Madison Columbus, 157
Robbins, Roswell Washington, 157
Robbins, William McKindy, 157
Roberson, Mrs. R. R., 150
Robert E. Lee, Gen., 144
Roberts, Mrs. F. C., 15, 107–9, 136, 148–49
Robertson, Mrs. Lucy H., 33
Robertson, Margaret (Mrs. Robert Burwell), 38
Robeson County, N.C., 162
Rockfish community of Cumberland and Hoke Counties, N.C., 47, 95
Rockingham County, N.C., 162
Rocky Point, N.C., 126
Roman, Capt. (nephew of Gen. Blount), 36
Ross, Capt. Edgar, 143
Roulhac, Miss Annie, 32
Roulhac, Mrs. Kate, 32

Round Knob community, N.C., 88
Roundtree, Mrs. Robert, home of, 66
Roundtree, Rose (Mrs. William Kennedy), 66
Rowan Artillery, 136
Rowan County, N.C., 90–91
Rowe, Mrs. Elizabeth Hoke, 160
Rowland, Dr. Dembar, 118
Ruffin, Mrs. May, 162
Ruffin, Thomas, 32
Rutherfordton, N.C., 160
Ryan, Father Abram, 103

Sadler, Miss (of Charlotte), 143
St. Bartholomew's Church, Pittsboro, 112
St. James Episcopal Church, Wilmington, 28, 112
St. John's Episcopal Church, Fayetteville, 111
St. Mary's School (Raleigh), 72, 105, 127–29
St. Paul's Episcopal Church, Edenton, 83–84, 112
Salem (Old Salem), N.C., 74, 139; boarding school, 105
Salisbury, N.C., 90–91, 92, 100–102, 130–31, 135–36
Sampson County, N.C., 63–64; 64–65, 125
Sanders, Miss Bertie, 150
Sanders, Mrs. Mary F. (Mrs. James M. Stevenson), 27
Sassacus (Federal gunboat), 84
Saunders, Mrs. Lucien, home of, 64
Schofield, (U.S.) Gen., 27, 69
Scholar's Companion, The (textbook), 130
Scotland County, N.C., 153
Scotland Neck chapter, U.D.C., 85
Scott, Mrs. W. W., 90
Scott, Mrs. W. W., Jr., mother of, 90
Seagle, Andrew Jackson, 159
Seagle, Benjamin Franklin, 159
Seagle, Mrs. Daniel, 158
Seagle, James Monroe, 158
Seagle, Martin Van Buren, 159
Seagle, Nathaniel Macon, 159
Seagle, Polk Dallas, 159
Seagle, Thomas Jefferson, 158
Shaffuer, Miss Sarah E., 139
Sharon (home of Dr. Jonathan North), 94

Sharp, Lt. Col. Thomas, 78
Sharpe, Henry Clay, 163
Sharpe, Mrs. Jacob (Elizabeth), 163
Sharpe, Thomas, 163
Sharpe, William, 163
Shaw, Rev. Colin, 93
Shaw, Miss Margaret, 96
Shaw, Miss Mollie, 93
Shelby, N.C., 138
Shepherd, Miss Kate (Mrs. Col. Risden Tyler Bennett), 39
Sherman, (U.S.) Gen. William T., 47–49, 50, 53–54, 63–64; 64–65, 71–72, 73, 95, 97, 129, 145; soldiers, 56
Shobert, Mrs. Frank, home of, 92
Simpson, Benjamin Franklin, 153
Simpson, Faucette, 153
Simpson, George Washington, 153
Simpson, Haywood, 153
Simpson, Henry Jackson, 153
Simpson, James Ruffin, 153
Simpson, Jefferson, 153
Simpson, Lemuel, 153
Simpson, Mrs. Lemuel (Lucy Faucett), 153
Simpson, Martin Van Buren, 153
Simpson, William, 153
Simpson, Wyatt, 153
Skinner, Capt. T. L., 82
Slocumb, Mrs. John, 35
Smedes, Dr. Albert, 128
Smith, Miss (of Asheville), 136
Smith, Alex, 155
Smith, Curtis, 155
Smith, Douglas, 155
Smith, Edward, 155
Smith, Col. Ezekiel Smith, 155
Smith, Mrs. Fannie Browning, 162
Smith, Farquhard, 155; family of, 53–55; home of, 55
Smith, Mrs. Farquhard, 155; home of, 54–55
Smith, Gen. W. A, 134–35
Smith, Gen. William A., 60–62
Smith, Henry, 155
Smith, James, 155
Smith, Miss Janie, 150
Smith, Mrs. J. C., 150
Smith, Jesse Slocumb, 155
Smith, Miss Jessie Slocumb, 54, 149–51

Smith, John, home of (Oak Grove), 53–54, 150; family of, 53–55
Smith, Miss Kate, 134–35
Smith, Miss Lena H., 85
Smith, Miss Louise, 150
Smith, Mary Slocumb (wife of Col. Ezekiel Smith), 155
Smith, Maj. Orren Randolph, 132–34
Smith, Miss S. E., 150
Smith, Miss Sallie, 150
Smith, Mrs. J. Henry, 68
Smith, Mrs. Lewis, 158
Smith, Orren R., 40
Smith, Peter E., 85
Smith, Robert Lawson, 162
Smith, William, family of, 53–55; home of, 54
Smithfield, N.C., 64
Smithville community, N.C., 55
Smithville Memorial Association, 150–51
Smyre, Mrs. Katherine Fry, 160
Social Reminiscences of Noted North Carolinians (Clarke), 103
Soldier's Aid Society (of Louisburg), 40
Soldier's Aid society (of Old Salem), 74
Soldier's Aid Society of Charlotte, 37
Soldier's Home (Raleigh), 148
Soldiers' Aid Society (of Hillsborough, N.C.), 33–34
soldiers' aid society (of Orange County, N.C.), 32
Soldiers' Aid Society, Wilmington, 26, 27, 146
Soldiers' Relief Association of Rowan County, 91
Southerland, Mrs. W. T., 140
Southern Memorial Association, 167
Spannor, Capt., 36
Spear, Mrs. Maria, 145–46
Spencer, Mrs. Cornelia Phillips, 98–100
Spottswood, Miss Mary, 85
Sprunt, Dr. James, 41
Stallings, Mrs. Richard, 158
State Medical Department (Wilson), 50, 79
State Soldiers' Home (Raleigh), 50
Statesville, N.C., 92, 114, 162
Stedman, Miss (of Fayetteville), 124
Stedman, Joe, 160
Stedman, John, 160

Stedman, Josh, 160
Stedman, Mrs. Sophia Stedman (widow), 160
Stedman, Townsend, 160
Stedman, William, 160
Stephens, Alexander, 69
Stephens, widow (of Buncombe County), 155
Stevenson, Mrs. David, 157
Stevenson, Maj. James M., 27
Stevenson, Mrs. James M., 27
Stinson, Mrs. Nancy, 154
Stockard, Henry Jerome, 175–76
Stone, Albert, 158
Stone, Atlas, 158
Stone, Jackson, 158
Stone, Mrs. Jonathan M. (Rebecca Jane), 158
Stone, Marion, 158
Stone, Rufus, 158
Stone, Silas, 158
Stoneman, (U.S.) Gen., 86, 89–90, 91
Stratford, Mrs. Jane Cooper, 157
"Stuart Leigh" (pseud. of Mary Bayard Clarke), 103
Suggs, Mrs. Minnie (as young girl in Kinston), 57–58
Swepsonville, N.C., 69

Tarboro, N.C., 43, 112, 137, 149, 163
Tatum, Alexander, 156
Tatum, Gray, 156
Tatum, Hanson, 156
Tatum, Jonathan, 156
Tatum, Marshal, 156
Tatum, Mrs. Olive, 156
Tatum, Richard, 156
Tatum, Simeon, 156
Taylor, Dorsey, 163
Taylor, Miss (of Fayetteville), 124
Taylor, Mrs. Alexander, 15, 16
Taylor, John, 163
Taylor, Lafayette, 163
Taylor, Mrs. Sophia, 163
"Tenella" (pseud. of Mary Bayard Clarke), 103
Terry, Gen., 71
Thenie, maid in Holt household, Lexington, 123

Thomas, Mrs. Robert (Mary Lewis), 154
Tiernan, Mrs. Frances Fisher ("Christian Reid"), 100–102, 177–78
Tillinghast, Miss Sarah Ann, 21–23, 95, 103, 171–72, 174
"To Mothers of the U.D.C." (poem), 119
Tolar, Alfred, 154
Tolar, Haynes, 154
Tolar, John R., 154
Tolar, John, 154
Tolar, Joseph, 154
Tolar, Matthew, 154
Tolar, Robert, 154
Tolar, Mrs. Robert (Fannie Autry), 154
Tolar, Sampson, 154
Tolar, Thomas, 154
Tolar, William, 154
Topic (newspaper, Lenoir, N.C.), 90
Tredegar Iron Works (Richmond, Va.), 33
Trenton, N.C., 19, 161

U.S. Arsenal, Fayetteville, N.C., 21
Union church, Weldon, N.C., 112
United Confederate Veterans, 160; N.C. Division, 60, 134, 164
Union County, N.C., 158
Union Ridge, N.C., 162, 163
United Daughters of the Confederacy, 167; Memorial Hall (Stone Mountain, Ga.), 104; *see also* N.C. Division, U.D.C., and references to individual chapters
University of North Carolina, 99–100

Valerie Aylmer (novel), **102**
Vance, Gov. Zebulon B., 98, 116
Vance, Mrs. Zebulon, 114
Vaughn, Mrs. (of Lenoir), 90

Wachovia Historical Society (Winston-Salem), 139
Waddell, Mrs. A. M. (Gabrielle DeRosset), 42–43
Waddell, John, 135
Wadesboro, N.C., 39, 62, 73, 135
Wake County, N.C., 31, 147–48, 151–52, 158
Walker, John, 163
Walker, Joshua, 163
Walker, Mrs. Lettie, 68–69

Walker, Mrs. Lucinda, 163
Walker, William, 163
Warren County, N.C., 144–45, 160, 161, 163
Warrenton, N.C., 104
Washington Grays, 136
Washington, D.C., 44
Washington, N.C., 35–36, 124, 136, 136–37; churches, 111
Wataugua County, N.C., 92
Watson, Rev. A. A., 27
Watson, Albert, 160
Watson, Mrs. Allison Lee (Elizabeth Yarborough), 159
Watson, Archibald, 160
Watson, Charles, 160
Watson, Haywood, 160
Watson, James, 160
Watson, Miss Winnie, 134–35
Watters, Mrs. (of Washington), 137
Wayne County Female Academy, 140
Wayside Hospital (Rowan County), 91
Weaver, Mrs. Amos (Caroline Louisa Tomlinson), 159, 161
Weaver, Franklin Harrison, 159
Weaver, Franklin, 161
Weaver, George Washington, 159
Weaver, George Washington, 161
Weaver, Henry Clay, 159
Weaver, Preston DeKalb, 159
Weaver, Preston, 161
Weaver, Romulus Lafayette, 159
Weaver, Rufus, 161
Webb, Miss (of Bertie County), 137
Webb, Mr. Tom, 32
Weldon, N.C., 77–78, 112; church, 78
Wharton, Capt. Rufus, 139
Wheeler's Calvary, 64
White, Mrs. Murdock, 64–65
White, Mrs. William (Sarah Wilson), 38, 158
Whitehall, N.C., 35
Whitehead (Federal gunboat), 84
Wiggins, (U.S.) Maj. (of Ohio), 142
Wiggins, Alfred, 156
Wiggins, Blake, 156
Wiggins, Elizabeth Slade (Mrs. Mason L.), 141
Wiggins, Eugene, 156

Wiggins, John, 156
Wiggins, Mason L., 141
Wiggins, Mrs. Mason Lee (Elizabeth Slade), 156
Wiggins, Octavius, 156
Wiggins, Thomas, 156
Wiggins, William, 156
Wiley, Rev. Calvin H. (state superintendent of common schools), 106
Wilfong, Charles, 159
Wilfong, Henry, 159
Wilfong, John, 159
Wilfong, Mrs. John, 159
Wilfong, Milton, 159
Wilfong, Pinkney, 159
Wilfong, Sidney, 125
Wilfong, Sidney, 159
Wilkes County, N.C., 162
Wilkes, Mrs. John, 37
Wilkins, Mrs. Ida, 77–78
Williams, A. H. A., 157
Williams, Mrs. F. M., 117
Williams, Mrs. Fannie Ransom, 118
Williams, Harry, 161
Williams, Mrs. Henry G., 157
Williams, James, 161
Williams, John, 157, 161
Williams, Mrs. John Buxton, 161
Williams, Mrs. Julia J., 150
Williams, L. S. (father of Mrs. J. P. Caldwell), 143
Williams, Lucy (Mrs. Polk), 145
Williams, Samuel, 157
Williams, Col. Solomon, 157, 161
Williams, Thomas, 157
Williams, William, 157
Wilmington, N.C., 12, 26–31, 66, 94, 118, 146–47, 163; churches, 27–28, 112
Wilson Light Infantry, 79
Wilson, N.C., 79, 134, 160
Winborne, Mrs. [Benjamin?] (Rebecca Murphy), 40, 132–34
Windsor, N.C., 40, 137; church, 137
Winnie Davis Chapter, U.D.C., 154
Winston, Francis, 129
Winston, Judge Francis, 40
Winston, Mrs. Patrick Henry, 40, 137
Winston-Salem, N.C., 139

"Woman of the Confederacy, The" (poem), 175–76
Woodbury, (U.S.) Gen., 30
Woodfin, Miss Anna, 136
Woodfin, Mrs. Nicholas, 88
Woodlawn (home of Mrs. Elizabeth Slade Wiggins, Halifax County, N.C.), 141, 156
Wood-notes: Carolina Carols (comp. Clarke, 1854), 103
Wooten, Allen, 160
Wooten, Anna Jones, 132
Wooten, Edward, 160
Wooten, John, 160
Wooten, Lewis, 160
Wooten, Mrs. Mary Eliza, 160
Wooten, Oscar, 160
Worth, Bettie (Mrs. Henry A. [London]), 73
Worth, Gov. Jonathan, 73
Worth, Lucy (Mrs. John Jackson), 73
Worth, Miss Nellie (Mrs. George French), 65, 94
Worth, Mr. Jonathan, 115–16
Worth, Mrs. Jonathan, 115–16
Wrenn, Miss Betty (daughter of Mary A. Wrenn), 91
Wrenn, Mrs. Mary A., 91
Wyhisine (Federal gunboat), 84

Yancey, George, 163
Yancey, Henry, 163
Yancey, John, 163
Yancey, Mrs. Tempe Boddie, 163
Yeopin Creek, Cedar Vale, N.C., 80
Young Ladies Knitting Society (Fayetteville), 25
Young Ladies' Seminary (Fayetteville), 46
Young Woman's Knitting Society (Fayetteville), 24

www.ingramcontent.com/pod-product-compliance
Lightning Source LLC
Chambersburg PA
CBHW030442300426
44112CB00009B/1122